# Hands That Made Lights Work

## A Lighthouse Keeper's Essay

Gordon Partridge

authorHOUSE®

*AuthorHouse™ UK Ltd.*
*500 Avebury Boulevard*
*Central Milton Keynes, MK9 2BE*
*www.authorhouse.co.uk*
*Phone: 08001974150*

*First published by AuthorHouse 1/4/2010*

*ISBN: 978-1-4490-6613-0 (sc)*

*This book is printed on acid-free paper.*

# CONTENTS

# INTRODUCTION

Born in Brixham, South Devon, my family for generations, have been actively involved in the sea and commercial fishing; an industry for which Brixham has become justifiably reknowned.

Following a career at sea in various capacities, I, at aged 25, joined the Trinity House Lighthouse Service as a Supernumerary Assistant Keeper, (SAK), this being the training rank. I remained in service for some 22 years until the automation of Lighthouses forced my redundancy in 1996; the last remaining UK Lighthouse becoming demanned and automated in 1998.

This is my story, based upon my life and experiences in the Lighthouse Service; in it, I have attempted to provide an insight into the life of the Lighthouse Keepers, and how the Lighthouse Service functioned at the "tall" end. I began initially, to write what has turned into a somewhat prolonged essay, simply, a personal project, whilst on duty at Lizard Lighthouse, Cornwall, just three years before the silicon chips of computer control assumed the role of Keepers. In the years following, I have expanded upon my original, on watch notes, as recollections come to mind.

I hope that my story will serve to answer a few questions about the life and duties of the Lighthouse Keeper, and that you will enjoy sharing just a little of that life with me in the pages that follow. Some lights have become legendary, and are known, at least by name, to many, I refer to Lighthouses such as Wolf Rock, Eddystone, others. It is to be remembered, however, that each and every Lighthouse station is equally as important to safe sea navigation, and therefore each has played an equal part in our country's maritime history. I like to think that I, and all others in the Trinity House Lighthouse Service, have contributed, each in our own humble way towards being a part of that history.

My service duties took me to a variety of Lighthouses, both on, and off ,shore, but it is the latter category which has played the largest part in my service years, and in my deep appreciation and experiences as a serving Lighthouse Keeper.

On a personal note, my first ever duty was at Start point Lighthouse, near my home in South Devon; it was off this station, that one of our family trawlers, the "Cariad," was sunk by a U Boat during first world war hostilities; fortunately with no loss of life, the crew, led by my Great uncle Sam, were given just 10 minutes in which to take to their lifeboat.

I thank, and dedicate this work to, my wife Stella, without whose loyal support and encouragement, I would not have been able to follow, the career I so enjoyed, and, in which, I was proud to serve.

# PREFACE

I have written the following, very much in the form of an extended essay, in words "straight from the head," this, with two main motives in mind, and from my long held joy in writing.

Primarily, I have recorded the enclosed, very much as a personal project, in order that those who follow me will know a little of life within a manned Lighthouse. For the second part, it has been a pastime indulgence during those long, dark hours, of a duty watch, so often the time of self reflection and thought. I frequently felt that, during such solitary, often stormy, nights on watch, that one was warmly accompanied by the spirits of those, who in times past, had occupied that same space, and shared the same responsibilities. It was their examples of vigilence that we were endeavouring to follow, and whose dedication to service we hoped to emanate.

Prior to my joining the Lighthouse Service, despite having sighted many such stations at sea, I admit to having had certain perceptions as to how they functioned from within, and feel that such, often misguided, perceptions are shared by many.

I have learnt that the Lighthouse Keeper is no more or less anti social, introvert or eccentric, than anyone else within the population; in short, his views and attitudes towards life are just as with most; it is simply his workplace and his method of "travel to work" that makes his life a trifle unique!

Within the confines of a Lighthouse, there existed a kind of immunity from the less desirable aspects of so called "normal life." No traffic fumes, crime, or the often, unwanted speed at which outside life travels, and those caught within it, have little choice but to follow. To be free from all the more negative aspects of modern life must be the wish and envy of many, yet this, at least for part of the time, was the lot of the Lighthouse Keeper. Add to this, the daily experience of nature at first hand, and the almost unlimited opportunity for personal studies or hobbies, and lighthouse life shows itself to be an attractive proposition to even the more sceptical!

It has not been my intention to duplicate already well documented, history of Lighthouses, or to replicate works on their construction, all of which have, many times, been well recorded. I hope, however, to perhaps bring to question or change, perhaps a few misconceptions regarding the life of the Lighthouse Keeper. This is my story, based upon my own experiences within the Lighthouse Service that I have been proud to serve.

Gordon Partridge. Trinity House Lighthouse Service 1974-1996

Trinity House is the authority responsible for all Lighthouses, Lightvessels and Navigational Aids in England,Wales, Channel Islands & Gibralter.

Granted their original Charter in 1514, by Henry V111 th, the organisation is the oldest remaining Institution in England; predating Parliament and the Church of England.

# SECTION ONE
# THE LIGHTHOUSE EXPERIENCE

LIGHTHOUSES ATTENDED IN MY SERVICE OF TRINITY HOUSE.

| | |
|---|---|
| START POINT, S.DEVON. | Land |
| ANVIL POINT, DORSET. | Land |
| PORTLAND BILL, DORSET. | Land |
| ST CATHERINES, ISLE OF WIGHT | Land |
| DUNGENESS | Land |
| PENLEE POINT, E.CORNWALL | Land |
| LIZARD | Land |
| PENDEEN, N.CORNWALL | Land |
| TREVOSE HD. | Land |
| INNER DOWSING TOWER | N.SEA. Rock |
| FLATHOLM, BRISTOL CHAN. | Rock |
| LONGSHIPS, CORNWALL | Rock |
| BISHOP ROCK, SCILLY IS. | Rock |
| ROUND ISLAND, SCILLY IS. | Rock |
| WOLF ROCK, CORNWALL. | Rock |
| NEEDLES, ISLE OF WIGHT. | Rock |
| NAB TOWER, ISLE OF WIGHT. | Rock |
| LES CASQUETS, CHANNEL IS. | Rock |
| LES HANOIS, CHANNEL IS. | Rock |
| ALDERNEY | Rock |

# ABBREVIATIONS & TERMS USED IN LATER PAGES

TH.  Trinity House.

THLS. Trinity House Lighthouse Service

LV. Light Vessel. (Stationed where not practicable to erect Lighthouse)

P.K.  Principal Keeper. (Officer appointed responsible for Lighthouse)

A.K.  Assistant Keeper.  (Appointed assistant to PK)

SAK. Or "SUPER," Supernumarary Assistant Keeper. (Keeper in training)

RK.  Rock Lighthouse

LS.  Land Station Lighthouse.

THV.  Trinity House Vessel (Prefix given to ships name)

FS.  Fog Signal.

E.B.  Elder Brethren (The Governing Board of Trinity House)

*START POINT LIGHTHOUSE FROM SEAWARD 1975*

*THE LIGHTHOUSE KITCHEN, START POINT.*

Having the opportunity to join Trinity House as a Lighthouse Keeper, was, for me, something of an adventure; I knew very well, as a seafarer, the need for Lights, and appreciated, at least, some of the difficulties that must prevail in keeping them in the A1 reliable category of Navigational Aids that their reputation had bestowed upon them. What I did not really know, was just what went inside, or indeed just how the system in control worked! I knew, of course, that there was a crew inside every Lighthouse, but wondered just what type of person would place themselves in such an isolated and potentially dangerous situation, and of who does what in the crew structure. I only knew with certainty, that having seen first hand from the seaward perspective, just what conditions of weather they had to endure, that there must be a strong sense of duty and dedication amongst the Keepers. I admired their tenacity in the wish to assist in the safety of others at sea. Put quite simply, when most vessels go running for shelter, the Lighthouses and Lightvessels are always out there, shining out their reassuring warning signals. With all this in mind, and having completed the appropriate application forms, I found myself being invited to London, to Trinity House itself!

Trinity House stands upon Tower Hill, literally just across from the Tower of London, it stands, impressively, complete with gleaming cannons, as an almost guardian sentinel overlooking the River Thames. I felt so proud to just be there, and even more so to think that I might fairly soon, and with luck, become a part of the organisation that boasts this most impressive of Headquarters. Once having entered, I quickly discovered that the interior was as inspiring and steeped in our country's maritime history as the frontage had suggested, and, he was I, this relatively young man from a Devon fishing family, here by invitation! My immediate thought was, that, even if, for whatever reason, I am not deemed suitable to join Trinity House, then it would still have all been worthwhile even to simply enjoy the maritime ambience of this, one of our history's oldest Corporations.

Later in the day, having sat, and happily passed, various tests and preliminary interviews etc, I was further interviewed by a Mr

Peter Edwards, Trinity House Welfare and Personnel Officer, and felt immediately at ease in his company. He proceed to tell me that, he himself was a former Lighthouse Keeper, and had served in various offshore tower Lighthouses, naming the Longships, Cornwall, as one example. I later learned that, he was, in fact, the only member of staff within the Tower Hill establishment that had actually served time in a real Lighthouse! This information, meant a lot to me, in as much that I was actually dealing with someone who had served at the "sharp end " and who was therefore speaking with much credibility. It also said much about the organisation itself; that such promotion and opportunity was open to all within it's ranks.

Following a lengthy interview, throughout which, much emphasis was placed of the need for self reliance in both attitude and ability, and after an exam, I was then dispatched across London to attend a Medical Assessment, but not before I enquired of Mr Edwards as to my chances thus far. He replied with a smile and a polite nod, all unofficial, but nonetheless reassuring to me! Later, returning homewards on the train, I felt highly pleased with my mission to the capital!

Following what felt like the longest three weeks of my life, my letter of appointment arrived, I was in! I would be serving as a Supernumerary Assistant Keeper in the East Cowes, (Isle of Wight), District, further instructions to follow!

I joined the service in May 1975 and was instructed to join Start point lighthouse for induction and basic training prior to formal training at Blackwall on the next available intake course. Invaluable as the Training School was, in laying the foundation for duty in real Lighthouses, the "hands on" experience of the SAK played an equally valid role.

For administrative purposes, Trinity House's nationwide jurisdiction was sub divided into four "districts" of which "my district," East Cowes, was the largest in area and Lighthouse numbers.

East Cowes District included all stations west of a line from Dungeness (Kent), to Hartland Point (N.Devon), and encompassed the

Channel Islands, Isles of Scilly, and Gibraltar. This therefore included some of the most famous and well known Lighthouses; Eddystone, Wolf Rock, Needles, and more. Other "districts were administered from Harwich (Essex), Holyhead (Anglesey), and Swansea (S.Wales). Each district office was known as a Trinity House Depot, and was a self contained unit with stores and maintenance workshops sufficient to service the "day to day" requirements of the stations within it's remit area. Each Depot had a District Superintendent , with the rank of Captain, in overall charge. The District Superintendent was responsible for, and would regularly inspect, all of the stations within his District area.

In addition to admin units, each Depot had a fully functioning Wharf from where Trinity House Vessels (THV's) would take on stores etc, for delivery to off shore Lighthouses and Lightvessels; they would also load, or discharge for servicing, Navigation Buoys used in marking major shipping lane hazards, e.g. Sandbanks etc. THV,s would also embark Lighthouse and Lightvessel crews before setting off to stations in order to effect "reliefs" of stations within a given area. ("Relief" was the term used throughout the Service for crew change overs ) At the time of my entry into the Service, there were five Trinity House Vessels in the Corporation fleet; in later years, with the increased use of helicopters, the Vessel fleet was gradually reduced.

Reliefs were also carried out by contracted "local Boatman," who, as their title suggests, were experienced locals who intimately knew their sea area, in particular, waters and hazards surrounding their contracted Lighthouse area. Many local boatman's families had carried out this work, on behalf of Trinity House, for many generations. Many such Boatmen were fishermen who saw, almost on a daily basis, just what conditions could be like, and how they often deteriorate or even improve around the lighthouse landing area, at any given state of the tide. Each individual lighthouse had it's own ideal state of tide during which a relief might best be attempted; such windows of opportunity only prevailing for sometimes less than an hour during bad winter weather.

The expression, "fair weather window" soon becoming a phrase I heard often throughout my service!

Trinity House also operated a major maintenance workshop situated at Blackwall, E.London, (now the site of the London Docklands development complex). Within Blackwall workshops equipment of all kinds was manufactured, in addition to which, equipment from Lighthouses and Lightvessels was serviced, repaired, and sent back to station to be installed by Blackwall's "out station" team. These were tradesmen Mechanics, Electricians and others who stayed aboard the Lights, often for several weeks at a stretch, completing the task that their workshop colleagues had started on the workbench. It was often said that, if it could not be repaired at Blackwall, then it simply was not repairable!

It is to Blackwall, that all newly appointed Lighthouse Keepers would come, as it was here that the Trinity House Training School was located, and we would be taught, and examined on, all the basic skills necessary to life aboard a lighthouse.

I arrived at Start Pt on a wet, foggy morning, the Fog Horn sending out it's mournful, almost deafening greeting posing me momentary serious personal questions regarding my career choice ! The warm greeting from the duty Keeper soon eliminated any misgivings!

All new entrants into Trinity House lighthouse service were required to undergo initial formal training at Blackwall Training School; such training involved operation and maintenance of all navigational equipment common to lighthouses, ( Main Lights, Fog Signals etc), Diesel Generator/Alternator Sets, and Radio Beacons. By the end of the one month intensive course, each student would leave the school having attained a Certificate of Competency in Radio telephony with full authority to operate, Certificate of Qualification in First Aid at Sea (including use of dangerous drugs by injection), Meteorology Observing and general lighthouse management. In addition, basic ropework skills, splices, knotting etc were taught, essential for use in boatwork at offshore lighthouses; the latter subject being comfortably (smugly!) familiar to me thanks to my family seafaring background. All subjects were taught professionally, and with good humour by Instructors who had actually seen service, within their respective trade remits, on the very stations, whose operations, we would soon be experiencing ourselves first hand. For myself, their background of experience inspired me as they were teaching with a knowledge based upon their own service.

The Training School had it's very own lighthouse, building of some 20 metres height; within it were to be found a variety of illuminants, which even included oil burners. From the top of the tower we learned the only escape evacuation method for use in the event of a fire, and were reminded that a lighthouse is simply a chimney awaiting a fire!

In the event of evacuation, the method of escape was via the "Davy Fire Escape," a device which basically involved a rope down the side of the lighthouse tower. This equipment, by design, gently lowers a person of any given weight down the tower in a controlled and safe manner; it is made up of two harnesses with one harness ascending the tower empty, as the weighted one descends. It's top end is shackled to the lighthouse gallery and houses a geared ratchet reel which ensures a gentle descent for all; in practice, a novel experience, the most daunting part being the "letting go" prior to journeying downward. Once having completed the operation, and feeling quietly confident, everyone without exception, requested another go!

On completion of our training of Blackwall, further training and experience was gained by undertaking duty at various lighthouses, on and offshore, as needed, usually covering for the absence of a Keeper from his regular station. As we progressed, and following any tour of duty at a particular station, the Keeper in Charge was obliged to complete entries in our SAK Report Book, such entries included details regarding competence, training and attitude etc; copies of these reports were regularly forwarded to the District Superintendent for his examination.

Blackwall gave me the opportunity of seeing first hand, the range of skilled work being undertaken in the workshops, and made me realise just what was involved in keeping the lights around our coasts in their first class operating condition. Blackwall's skills were often requested by other authorities Worldwide, usually former British colonies, to assist and advise regarding maintenance works on their Lighthouses.

NB. A Lighthouse Gallery is the area surrounding the outside of the lantern.

Trinity House Lighthouse Service required that uniform clothing should be worn when on duty on station, or when "standing by" awaiting relief. Our uniform as Lighthouse Keepers was ,in many ways, not dissimilar to that worn by serving Royal Naval Petty Officers. It consisted of a Navy Blue Reefer Jacket and Trousers worn with a white shirt and black tie; upon the sleeves were warn seniority chevron flashes and on each shoulder, in gold thread, the words, "Trinity House". As an alternative, but not for formal occasions, a service style "woolley pulley" sweater could be worn with the dark trousers. A white officer style cap and black shoes completed the uniformed look. Photos of the author in uniform shown within this book add further description.

In addition to the more formal "number one" wear, work wear formed part of the uniform issue and consisted of a blue shirt to be worn with navy blue overall type trousers; this, during day to day duties on the lighthouse, was obviously much more practical. Just as with the Royal Navy, this "working uniform" was affectionately known as "eights;" the reason for this title is unknown to me!

Trinity House provided full uniform clothing and other personal issue requirements, i.e. towels, sea socks and any personal protective gear such as survival and storm suits.

It was a regulatory condition of service that all personnel should, at all times, be in possession of a full, good ordered number one uniform as a priority before any other items of issue. Every serving member of Trinity House Service was allocated a given number of uniform credit points to be "spent" when ordering ones' uniform requisites, with each individual item of clothing having an associated "points price." The annual point allotment for a member of the Lighthouse Service was

117 points, which, if not spent in any one year, would be credited to the following. For the number one uniform issue, self measurement forms were to be completed to enable each individual uniform to be personally made to measure by the supplier.

For engine room and similar duties, boiler suit coveralls and protective footwear also formed part of annual issue, although, as Health and Safety regulations dictated, then so issue of appropriate protective equipment was increased accordingly.

Prior to my service, I have to admit that my perception of a Lighthouse Keeper had been that of a grey bearded, perhaps chubby figure, in a dark blue uniform, which when worn with the customary sea socks and turned down "wellies," gave

Him an almost, "nautical Santa" appearance! This most always, seemed to be how a Keeper was portrayed within the media, and having never previously seen or met a "real Lighthouse Keeper" before joining, I had little choice but to continue my suspicious perception. How wrong I was! Speaking with others in the service, I discovered that, in the main, my miss perceived character was, in fact, a shared view!

Receiving my made to measure, spanking new uniform issue, I felt smart, proud, and a real part of Trinity House; being a Lighthouse Keeper, gave me a kind of unique identity amongst my friends at home, this identity, even long after the demise of such the career, seems to have stuck!

*THE AUTHOR IN NUMBER ONE DRESS UNIFORM.*
*NOTE SINGLE CHEVRON ON SLEEVE INDICATES*
*SEVEN YEARS SERVICE*

As one progressed through the Service, refresher courses became a frequent necessity as new equipment and technology was added to the stations in our charge; as helicopters took on an increasing role, this alone demanded that all involved became familiar with operating procedures.

SAK Service provided all new entrants with the best possible experience encompassing a wealth of different situations and problems; this could only realistically be achieved by personal duty in a "hands on" way. When on station, the SAK was an integral member of the crew of three Keepers, and shared the same duties and responsibilities. An SAK would usually be on station in place of a regular crew member who, for a variety of reasons might be absent, i.e sick or on leave

With each station and it's equipment varying from station to station, each new station offered a whole new process of learning. Whilst the basic methods of operating the navigational aids and their various standby systems might be, within reason, standard, one's first day or so on a new station required some tuition from the regular crew to ensure best operating confidence. At the time of my entry into the Service, almost all lights were electrically driven with the exception of Alderney, (Channel Is), which was still reliant on I.O.B (Incandescent Oil Burner). Within the first year of my service, this light also had been converted to electric power. In addition to learning station "light up" methods, there was still the Fog Signal equipment to master! This involved the use of diesel powered air compressors, electrical coding apparatus, and a lot of loud noise!

Starting the Fog Signal was the sole responsibility of the Keeper on watch, it was he who made the decision as to whether the visibility, or rather, the lack of it, demanded it's use. Each station had it's own "fog marks" from which determine the state of visibility; these could vary from an area of coastline, to a specially laid marker buoy, (as in case of Wolf Rock). At night, visibility was much more difficult to judge than during the day, and called for much more discretion. Under certain weather conditions, the beams from the main light could appear 'milky" which gave the impression that visibility was less than good; it was often the case, however, that at sea level, the horizontal range of visibility was, in fact, excellent, with ships lights shining brightly from many miles away. If, however, the beams reflected thick white light, and all light was being reflected back towards it's source, then it was more than time to get the noise operating! To achieve this, involved a very ordered routine, which needed to be adhered to in strict sequence order.

Step one involved starting usually, two diesel compressors, which once safely running, required opening a series of large wheel valves to allow the air into a storage receiver (tank).Once the receiver pressure gauge indicated sufficient pressure,(variable between stations), then the air could be released to the actual Fog Signal sounding tank which would enable the "noise" to begin. Frequency of sounding character was determined by a coding device which controlled air flow into the Fog Signal trumpets for several seconds in every minute. As with navigational lights, each station had it's own individual fog signal timing character for the purpose of recognition by mariners. There were several different sound types in use throughout the service, i.e. Supertyphon (Needles), Diaphone (Casquets) in addition to others, each emanating an individual sound type to assist recognition. This information is recorded on international marine charts to increase ease of identification, such charts being amended, and an official "Notice to Mariners" issued, as appropriate to change in Lighthouse navigational aid character.

Travelling from station to station, often with minimal or no leave in between, made life as an SAK quite difficult at times, but, with the benefit of hindsight, proved the most effective way of learning the Service and becoming aquainted with the pressures involved in trying to operate often "against the elements."

All Lighthouses were, in my experience, well equipped with reasonable quality "in house" amenities, i.e. televisions, radios, etc. "It wasn't always so!" the old hands would remind us, whilst admitting that, it was only moving with the times on the part of Trinity House. I felt that we were well catered for, and possibly even better off than some households ashore, particularly as all appropriate licence fees were met by Trinity House.

Television sets were black and white receivers, with the exception of sets on two Lighthouses; at Needles and Bishop Rock, the crews were able to enjoy full colour viewing! This, at a time when colour televisions were the reserve of the minority of the population! After service at either of these stations, television viewing at home seemed a bit of a climb down when sat in front our own black and white set! The privilege of "posh" viewing by certain lighthouse crews was, however, only brought about by the generosity of two outside organisations.

Needles Lighthouse was "adopted" by the nearby Royal Lymington Yacht Club who, throughout the year would collect for the Needles Lighthouse comfort fund. Their kindness was never more evident than at Christmas time when well stocked hampers of Festive Fayre would arrive on station courtesy of the Yacht Club. Accompanied by often, several hundred yachts, the local Lifeboat would call in just a few days prior to Christmas itself and deliver the packages, whilst the yacht crews would sing carols and signal greetings; this experience is one which, short of actually being there, is difficult to imagine, but leaves one with a memory which will never fade. This same kindness found us being presented with a colour television from all at the Club. Later gifts included a Music Centre and a large Deep Freeze; all such gifts benefiting all the station complement and raising living standards aboard the "Rock"

The appearance of Bishop Rock on television had much to do with their acquiring their very own new colour set. The well known children's television programme "Blue Peter" featured the Bishop and it's Keepers; Sony UK, noticing what they considered to be a much outdated TV Set on station, presented the Lighthouse with the latest in up market colour viewing! Whilst fully appreciating the kindness of provision of these colour sets by well meaning organisations, footing the extra licence bill fell to Trinity House, whom I am pleased to note, willingly accepted. Perhaps they felt that there was little choice! With Needles and Bishop each having new televisions, the added bonus to the crew meant use of the spare sets as an alternative to be taken elsewhere in the lighthouse for private viewing; whilst I never knew of any viewing choice fall outs among Keepers, no doubt the second set enhanced Lighthouse harmony!

Most Keepers, myself included, had a radio or cassette player in their bunk for private listening, a relaxing prelude to sleep when all outside was storm lashed and noisy, in which situation I always felt a certain smugness at being tucked up and warm, favourite music playing through the headphones in my own little private world!

Another old established Lighthouse comfort was the delivery of the Missions to Seamen Library box, each containing a selection of some fifty or so books. Each box would remain on station for up to three months, by which time all the contents had been read, and the box could be exchanged with another station. Once a group of Lighthouses had exhausted the library supply, then, from their HQ in London, other boxes would be despatched our way. At regular intervals    a questionnaire would afford us the opportunity of stating our particular reading interests; the Mission would then endeavour to seek out relevant books for our pleasure. In addition to their Library Service, the Mission would from time to time, forward us a selection of magazines etc. These would be new, unsold and unread copies, usually only a month out of date; to the readers on station they were a most welcome receipt. As in the case of the Library, every effort was made by the Mission to  supply magazines as appropriate to interest; I well remember a steam railway enthusiast  among us who regularly received his chosen subject reading courtesy of our Mission friends! Keepers themselves would take their favoured choice of reading, after which, the books would usually be left in the station's own "library" for all to enjoy.

All Lighthouse Keepers signed, upon joining, an agreement to serve wherever they were sent, be it on or offshore, the SAK however could, and was sent, to whatever Lighthouse needed his services, often at short, or no, notice. Duties at Land Stations was often less popular for the SAK than on any Rock, not least because Rock duty would only be for one month period, followed by the statutory one week off for "Supers;" Land station duty did not afford such a benefit, but instead, officially, was one day leave per each week on station. In fairness, the Officer in Charge of Cowes District, was always as kind as possible to myself and other SAK's in his charge, but, obviously, if circumstances dictate the need of a relieving Keeper somewhere, then somebody has to go ! I have personally, during one particularly busy period, served continuously for almost three months, travelling from station to station with no time off in between.

Life on a Rock Lighthouse meant sharing close quarter living with two other colleagues, with a possible extra complement of maintenance trades sharing the lighthouse space; lots of company, perhaps some good hands of cards etc whereas duty on a land station was for the SAK, myself included, often considered the "short straw."

Each shore station had well appointed, self contained accommodation for use of visiting personnel. Such quarters affectionately known as the "Supers, " could best be described as a flatlet with comfortable facilities, T.V. etc. Despite good comforts, duty on, particularly, certain land stations was not over popular.

Some Land Lighthouses lie within a relatively short strolling distance from the nearest village; stations such as Lizard (Cornwall), and St Catherines, (Isle of Wight), are two good examples from my own experience. There are, however, others, which, without any form of transport the relieving Keeper could, in effect, feel more isolated and alone than service on any rock. Good examples of such places are, amongst others, Start Point (Devon), and Trevose Head (Cornwall), each of which are some four miles or more from the nearest community or shop. Land station families had the benefit of a paid "shopping taxi" which visiting keepers were entitled to share; whilst many did, the general opinion seemed largely to be that it was often not in town long enough for one to really enjoy.

On a Land Station, the regular Keepers usually took their leave periods concurrently, with each taking perhaps 10 days each; the relieving Keeper (SAK) thereby having to spend a long period on station. Despite, on station there were two, or often three, other keepers on station, on a shore lighthouse, the regular crew lived on station with their families, whereas the SAK was alone. In my experience, the families always made the SAK more than welcome, and on many occasions one would be invited to share their kind hospitality for coffee, or even a meal; kindnesses for which I will always feel grateful, and which went a long way in preventing any feelings of solitude! Whilst personally, I have always felt myself a person well at ease with my own company, the comfort of a family, even if not one's own, was most welcome. To some new entrants, prolonged shore lighthouse duty, was more than they felt they could take, and consequently, felt unable to further persue the Lighthouse Keeper career. It was possible to take one's car to a land station, and several SAK's did so, the downside of such action meant that, if one was transferred at short notice to a Rock due to some emergency, one then had the added problem of just what to do with the car! I have known Keepers to have to "abandon" a car at the land station, then on completion of rock duty, have to travel miles back again to collect it, before proceeding home! With all public transport travel costs being met by Trinity House "in pursuance of duties," justifying one's car was impractical under most circumstances. Once, during my time as an SAK, I obtained permission from Trinity House for it,s use, only then because, during a public holiday, it was my only available method of travel in order to respond to an emergency. Trinity House then arranged for my car to be safely garaged in Penzance whilst I went on offshore duty.

Duty on an offshore rock, offered the SAK, a complete contrast of situation to that of duty ashore, not least in the constant personal companionship of two other Keepers. All duties, even to domestic arrangements, were a shared experience, and the congeniality of just having "company" went a long way in morale support! Add to this, the benefit of having a relief date which was only a month hence, and the differences are self explanatory! It was very rare, or only in exceptional emergency circumstances, that one did not proceed home on leave following rock duty; the entitlement of even only one week made off shore postings worthwhile when on route home on the train. All leave, however, for all ranks, was only granted "subject to the exigencies of the Service" (Quote. TH Regs)

Another attraction of rock service was obviously the extra premium salary allowances paid for simply being there. All Keepers received salary level as appropriate to rank, but, in addition, service offshore brought additional allowances paid, per day, of off shore service. Such payments included Rock Allowance and Victualling Allowance (payment towards food cost), and amounted to a much welcome enhanced salary cheque, following a period of duty off shore! Having joined the Service in May 1975, and having only served at only since, it was in January the following year that I received orders regarding my first visit to a "real" (offshore) Lighthouse!

My very first off shore experience was to be duty at Longships Lighthouse, approximately one and a half miles of Lands End, Cornwall, arguably the most post card featured off shore lighthouse in the service!

It was whilst doing relieving duty at Pendeen Lighthouse, (N.Cornwall ), that I formally received my instructions regarding Longships; I would be serving a full duty turn of one month duration. As an added "bonus," I was to be allowed a couple of days home leave prior to having to report to Trinity House Depot, Penzance, in order to organise the necessary stores etc . Duty on a Rock station, involved ensuring that everything one required for offshore duty was taken aboard, this obviously included foodstuffs and personal requisites; in a nutshell, whatever one had forgotten, one went without! No corner shop available on site!

It was most fortunate for me, that serving at Pendeen, were two Assistant Keepers, Christian names Fred and Brian, both of whom had, for several years previous, been stationed at Longships. They were most helpful in telling me everything and anything regarding life aboard, and were a great source of knowledge in advising me in just what type of foodstuffs, and how much, was essential for a months duty. They suggested the best shops in Penzance from which to pre order supplies, these were shops that they themselves had dealt with, and could be relied upon to deliver my order direct to Penzance Depot in readiness for packing. This to me, was an invaluable service, as the alternative would have involved doing the supermarket "trolley push," a prospect that I did not relish at all ! I will always be indebted to dear Fred and Brians' assistance, as, throughout my subsequent service career, that food list formed the model for all future offshore duties!

All outgoing Lighthouse crews were required to report to their muster point, i.e. Penzance Depot, by 1500 hours on the day prior to the actual relief; this was so as, QUOTE TH REGS "To be ready in all respects for their relief duty." On my arrival at the Depot, I was met with a hive of activity; the crews of four Lighthouses crews and one Lightvessel, were already busying themselves with the process of packing stores, provisions and personal gear. The relief, being via helicopter, meant that everything had be packed securely in purpose designed plastic containers, each of which had be individually weighed and logged for the attention of the Flight Crew, always remembering of course, to correctly label each container by name and Lighthouse in order to ensure correct address delivery!

Already at the Depot, and well ahead with their packing, were my two Longships Lighthouse fellow Keepers, to whom I was introduced; the Principal Keeper, Nat, and Assistant Keeper, Tim. I recall thinking ahead to just how much time we would be spending in each others' company, and of how pleased I felt with their congeniality!

Being aware that this was my first offshore duty, Nat immediately offered his help, enquiring as to whether I had been able to organise my food etc, whilst advising on the correct (and least breakable!) way of packing it all for despatch. Ever conscious and fearful at the possibility of running short of food, I invited Nat to look over my stores list and offer his opinion on choice and quantity. With an approving smile, he made comment that he was pleased to note that my stores list included a quantity of onions, as, in his words," we always like to have onions in our gravy" I felt immediately puzzled at his comment; I had never heard of nor experienced this apparent culinary Lighthouse favourite! To me, the thought of an onion bobbing about in the gravy boat was akin to a second world war mine floating in a very dark ocean! I kept my ignorance to myself, feeling that at some point, once out on the Lighthouse, the answer would soon reveal itself! Following further discussion regarding relief procedure and other service matters, I was then introduced to the Wharf Bosun, Walter, whose duty it was to ensure that everything and everybody on tomorrows relief schedule would be all in order to proceed and await instructions for the "off;" a visit to the Stores Officer was my last required port of call. From the stores, I was issued with a "Bed Bag," this being a kit bag in which were all necessary sheets, pillow cases and blankets essential to my offshore comfort. Upon coming ashore on relief, the bedding would all be despatched to the local laundry, along with the bedding from all the other stations within the group. From that point on, I was able to consider myself, "ready in all respects for relief." Following a quiet evening and a good night's sleep at the Hotel, the day arrived for my off shore adventure!

Presenting myself at Penzance Depot at 0830, I was soon in what was a convoy of taxis taking all the various crews to the Heliport . (Penzance), where we would embark via Trinity House own helicopter to our respective Lights. Our taxi convoy was followed by a large van containing the freight and foodstuffs that we had so industriously packed the previous day. Never before having ever flown in a helicopter, I admit to feelings of, almost childlike, excitement! Within a few minutes of my arrival at the Heliport, I was joined by my new found colleagues Nat and Tim, both of whom, living locally, had travelled direct from their homes

The van was soon unloaded and neat stacks of boxes were assembled by the ground crew, these were Depot staff who had undergone training in helicopter operations and the safe carriage of goods by air. Being a civilian airport, all operations came under the jurisdiction of the

Flight Controller, Penzance Heliport[1] who, by liason with our own Flight Marshall, oversaw all TH relief flights until operations were completed.

At 0930, our helicopter commenced with the first of the days, many relief flights with the first trip being out to Sevenstones Lightvessel (approx 12 miles from Lands End).This relief, unlike the Lighthouse Towers, was critically dependent upon good sea conditions to ensure that the ship maintained a stable platform on which to land. The Sevenstones relief having been completed, it was our turn, and I soon found myself overflying some of west Cornwall's beauty spots, the view of the clifftop perched Minack Theatre being particularly memorable. Leaving Lands End behind us, all too soon it seemed, we were landing on the Longships rooftop helipad; It was all over, just as I was beginning the ride! Our total flying time had only been for some fifteen minutes in total, Longships being the shortest flight path of all the group.

Bringing my thoughts back to reality, we were there to relieve three Keepers in order that they might get home on well deserved leave; with this in mind we were soon passing our gear down through the hatch to waiting hands, then in return, pulling up our colleagues baggage en route homewards. An exchange of life jackets, (compulsory when flying) and eager handshakes, we soon heard the roar of helicopter rotors and then they were gone, leaving us in relative silence. My first ever duty on an offshore lighthouse had begun!

The whole relief operation had, in total, taken only forty minutes, and we had arrived clean, dry, and looking our uniform best. What a contrast to times past when the only means of relief was by boat, in cold, wet, often dangerous conditions; little did I realise then that later in my career I would be able to add boat relief to my list of experiences! Anyway, we were on board, and all we had to do next was to get all the boxes etc from gallery level down into the Lighthouse; to add to the fun, when most towers were built, access was via the bottom door, hence the food storage and other lockers were all down in the lower sections some

six floors down! With helicopter reliefs arriving from the top,.........
it,s a long way down on stairways little more than step ladders! Before
commencing this heavy labour, it was time to collect our thoughts and
enjoy a coffee fresh from the pot left simmering on the stove for us by
the homeward crew, how thoughtful!

My new fellow Keepers soon directed me to my personal locker
space, fridges, and, most importantly, my bunk, shaped  like a banana
but home to me for the next four weeks! My having the top bunk, bed
making a banana shaped bunk with standard sized and shaped bedding,
is quite an experience when perched some five feet up a narrow ladder!
Once having settled in domestically, it was time for me to be trained
in all respects in the operations and working of station generators,
navigation light and fog horn. Until such training was initiated, no
"new" keeper could be deemed safe and efficient enough to cover a full
night watch without the benefit of supervision.

Fortunately, after a couple of hours training, and a few practice fog
horn blasts, I was judged by the Principal Keeper, (Nat) to present no
safety threat to world shipping if left in responsible charge on watch! It
was to be some three days later, before I needed to start the fog horn in
earnest, when as if to play "catch up," dense fog remained for 48 hours.
Living with the fog horns' blast, and the drone of the diesel compressors
was something that I admit not really being ready for, but realised that
it is simply not something one could ever imagine. Life in a tower, with
the fog horn sounding, was an experience on its' own; still, I thought,
if this is lighthouse keeping, I,d better get used to it!

"Getting used to it,' was the norm for me, certainly in my first few
days or so aboard the Longships; having found my way around, I was
shown the location of station stores, Explosives (Distress rockets)  and
other essentials, which included the First Aid and Dangerous Drugs
cabinets. With the station duty routine having been explained, I began
to feel a real part of the team. The station work routine was essential
to effective daily operation of the Lighthouse and its' systems; it was
the Keeper on the morning 0400-1200 watch that had most to do. A

Lighthouse Keepers first priority was to ensure that all navigational aids under his charge, were maintained in first class order of efficiency, this included ensuring that the main lens was kept scrupulously clean, this was attended to on a daily basis as soon as the light was extinguished. Other duties were as listed on Daily Routine Orders; I later learned that this same routine, with a few variations according to station, was common to all Lighthouses.[2]

Not fully knowing quite what to expect having only previously only served at shore stations, one of my first impressions was to just how small, internally, the Longships actually was. Longships Lighthouse had eight floors including the base door at almost at sea level, yet within that structure there were only two rooms for domestic use; most apace being given over to Engine Room, Fuel and other Stores, whilst the toilet was down adjacent to the base. The maximum diameter in any room was less than three metres, and with built in furnishings etc, available space in which to move around was even less. The bedroom, for example, had only two metres of free floor space at best; fortunately the skills of the Victorian builders had made best use of space beneath the bunks by building in lockers and drawers in a really inspiring way; their woodwork was superb.

In the kitchen, the second of only two "domestic rooms," when watching television,it was not possible to open the door without at least one other person having to move his chair! As appoint of note, I returned to Longships some six months later to find two additional personnel (Mechanics) on station; this was to turn daily living in a confined space into a Science. Confinement of space in rock towers was general within all such Lighthouses, with the problem being particularly acute at Longships, Wolf Rock, and Les Hanois. Service on an offshore tower called for a tidy and well ordered attitude in keeping the station in good, and Trinity House standard status; no room for leaving anything "not put away!" Nat, the PK, instilled this in me on the very first day of landing!

---

2

Privacy was limited on tower Lighthouses and the bunk was very much "one's world" wherein one could read, listen to radio or tape, or simply meditate and let the rest of the world outside, do its' own thing!

The routine on Longships revolved around watch keeping, catching up on sleep, and every third day, be duty cook, preparing the meal for all on station; this involved cooking meats provided by each individual keeper, and serving with a selection of ones' own vegetables from personal stock. Having a duty cook, served two purposes, "messing" in this way meant being able to have ones' meals cooked for two out of every three days, but equally importantly, owing to pure lack of space, having a single cook was much safer and practical than three men all vieing for "cooking space" at the same time! I was pleased that all on station seemed to enjoy my culinary offerings with clear plates at every meal. And the onion gravy ? Well, I need not have worried! It is nothing more than chopped onions boiled in a little water before adding in the gravy powder; the result, a highly onion enriched flavoured sauce with the main meal ;delicious with roast!

Despite lack of space, I was intrigued in just how little the full crew saw of one another, it being mainly during watch changes and mealtimes when all three were actually together. Living in such a closely confined space to fellow colleagues meant learning much, through conversation, about each others lives, dislikes, and service experiences. I learned that Principal Keeper Nat , was a Keeper with many years service behind him, whilst Assistant Keeper Tim, had only joined some two years previously; it was interesting to note that their attitudes to the Service were so vastly different. Nat, perhaps, was still running his station in much the same way as he had known since his formative Lighthouse years, and therefore had seemingly only embraced the changes that had been laid down in regulations and, as I heard said, on more than one occasion, "we've always done it that way." It was in only within two years prior to my tour of duty that it was possible to have a phone call, although via radio link courtesy of Lands End Coastguard, it at least enabled keepers to remain in contact with homes and families. This facility was shared between the five stations that made up the Lands End Group of lights, and as such, calls needed to be brief, but when compared days of old, new technology at its' best. Keepers at Longships, however, had devised, and were using, their very own means of communication, it allowed personal, and virtually private contact, between themselves and their families ashore; all that was needed was reasonably calm sea conditions, and good visibility. The outside wall surrounding the main doorway was painted white by the Keepers, who, when standing immediately in front of it, would semaphore messages to their watching families, who would be viewing via telescope from their cottages at Sennen, a mile and a half distant. The signalling Keeper, once having ended his "conversation," picking up his own telescope, would then view the reply from his family signalling from in front of the white walled cottage. It is well known that even the young children became very adept at signalling from a very early age, and much valued "talking to dad!" This facet of lighthouse life, has become a valuable, and little known part, of lighthouse social history.

I could not help but notice that were various tasks which clearly might have benefitted from a different, modern approach ,but realised that this was not Nat's way. Tims' views, on the other hand, seemed sometimes to me to be often too radical, and, whilst maybe offering an alternative point, I personally felt would not be conjusive to the Lighthouse service in which I was proud to be serving. These debates provided me with much lunch table entertainment to which I listened, but never got involved with except in the most neutral, polite fashion, taking much care in keeping my own real opinion to myself! I had no wish to be quoted, as I had the greatest respect for, in particular, Nat. The 1970's had seen major changes to the way that the Lighthouse Service operated, not least the reversion from two months on and one off to that of equal time on/off; this change had, apparently been opposed by many of the old school and had brought about an intake of new, younger Keepers in order to increase the man power necessary for the changes. New blood meant fresh ideas as to how to do things, and some of the older personnel had difficulty accepting change. Updating of new equipment meant new technology, again, often challenging the "ways we have always done it," and, in some cases, the ability of some in coping. For myself, I could see both sides of the debate, and whilst my fellow Longships Keepers continued in their "argument" I have to clearly state that it never got out of hand or personal, with each often agreeing to differ! Me? I remained 100% contented with the Lighthouse Service and its' traditions, and should I have ever been forced to voice a view, then I would have come down on the side of Nats' way rather than anything which questioned the Trinity House way; nothing radical for me !

I enjoyed my duty spell on Longships and felt that the experience had been of value in just how a Rock Lighthouse works, and just what is expected of its' crew. The month passed well, and apart from one day overdue thanks to dense fog, much to reflect upon.

I returned to Longships some six months later; a Keeper having been taken ashore sick, and I was to replace him on the crew; no helicopter for me on that occasion, my arrival being via local contract boat, following five days in Penzance awaiting the fair weather opportunity to effect a landing! Even on the day, the weather was less than good and a soaking provided me with my first boat christening! After that experience, I felt that my Longships CV was quite complete!

*LONGSHIPS LIGHTHOUSE FROM BOAT LANDING.*
*NOTE SMOOTH, FLUTED SHAPE OF LIGHTHOUSE TOWER*
*TO DEFLECT HIGH SEAS*

Taking up duty on an offshore station involved much personal preparation ,not least in insuring that medically,one could at least ,be as fit for the task as possible. when far from any hope of treatment; having seen colleagues suffer until arrangements could be made to evacuate the victim,it instilled a private dread within me,to avoid the experience at all costs!

One of the rulings within Trinity House, was, to ensure that one remained as dentally fit as could be maintained; to which I must add, that, only having been declared "dentally fit by my dentist the previous week, I still found myself in dire need of transfer ashore thanks to the ravages of toothache!

In addition to dental health, obviously on going offshore, remembering to pack any medication as appropriate is also a wise idea!


A typical watch for daylight hours mainly involved, particularly on the morning watch, routine duties as per standing orders, in addition to a visual lookout for impending poor visibility.

Every three hours, the station log had to be completed, such entries included the state of the weather, sea state, cloud cover and range of visibility, plus any incidents within the station area.; this was a legal document requiring the duty keepers signature to each of his entries. At the end of each day, the completed page was countersigned by the Principal Keeper/Officer in Charge and a copy taken for forwarding to Trinity House at next relief. Also reported in the log were any arrivals or departures of personnel, i.e. Mechanics or other visiting maintenance trades e.t.c Weather reports entered in the station log were not as comprehensive as in the case of the meteorological journal; this demanded a full weather observation which included cloud types and height, barometric readings and tendency (i.e falling or rising),wind direction and speed,( by anemometer), visibility and a range of thermometer readings .This was, not only recorded on an hourly basis in a log book, but was transmitted at prearranged times to a shore station, from whence it would be collated and passed on to the then weather headquarters at Bracknall. During the shipping forecast, some stations present weather was transmitted on a regular basis, i.e Royal Sovereign, Lundy, and others.Weather observations played a significant role in a keepers watch hours, as, by the time one "met ob" had been collated and sent, it was soon time for the next.

During darkness hours, it was a requirement of the watchman to ensure that the navigation light stayed in character, with the revolving lens, this was achieved by the timing of a revolution by stopwatch. Occulting lights, of which there were a few, i.e Needles, Longships, it was simply a case of recording the flash sequence timing.

Watches on station obviously involved having sleep and eating patterns being fairly erratic at times.Within the service, being on station be it on or off watch, meant being available to assist with any required task needing attention. The agreement whereby offshore rock stations were granted month on/off status was that all on station would be available as and when the need arose.

Following a morning watch (0400-1200),it was usual for a Keeper to "turn in", as it was known,for an hour or two, the main reason for this being that,having been called out at 0345,and later that day having to serve another 4 hours on 2000-2400 watch, one could begin to feel very tired well before the watch ended.I have known a few keepers who did not follow this routine,but,in my experience, the majority did. Personally,! enjoyed my watch keeping hours,not least because, having rested,I felt fresh,alert,and better able to deal with any eventuality.

Another traditionally grabbed period of rest preceded the 0000-0400 watch, commonly called,"the middle".On that particular watch day,one would have served 1200-2000,and,later, during the four hour off period, getting some sleep ensured a relatively easy watch time.

Call out times for night or morning duties was always 15 minutes before start time,(quarter to the hour);having awoken the next duty watchman,one would then proceed to make him a pot of tea or coffee. On stations undertaking meteorology readings on the hour,it was usual to carry out this task for ones on coming colleague,so as,at least,he would have an hour before having to go outside and take cloud, wind readings etc,which,when having just arisen from bed,would not have been a deal of fun!Also,perhaps when not fully awake,it may not have been too wise to venture outside the lighthouse!

It was not uncommon,during watch hand overs,for the now off duty keeper,to stay up for quite some time before turning in to bed. During such times,and in good conversation,one found out much about ones'colleagues and their lives outside the lighthouse.From such,came good companionship and,often,lifelong friendships.Despite three men living in such close proximity to one another inside a slender tower,one saw surprisingly little of one another during day to day operations;there almost always being a keeper in bed between watches,and another busying himself with the designated duty of the day; the third man,would be in the kitchen as cook of the day! At about 1100,it was usual for the cook to serve morning coffee, as, by then, all the crew would be around.

One major reason for one person to be responsible for the days meals, this tending to be the keeper who was on the "day of",24 hour watch free period, was simply that, in tower rock kitchens, space was very limited, it being therefore much easier and safer if one person alone did the catering for all three crew. The cook of the day would also do all of the clearing and washing up, meaning that, for two days out of every three, one had no culinary responsibilities whatsoever. Most of us agreed that we did much more when we were at home!

# WATCHKEEPING HOURS, 3 HANDED STATIONS

DAY ONE: 0400-1200 & 2000-2400
DAY TWO: 1200-2000 & 0000-0400
DAY THREE: NO WATCHES, BUT ANY OTHER DUTIES


## LIGHTHOUSE SERVICE MORNING WATCH ROUTINE.
### (AS TYPICAL )

Daily.

Extinguish Light(s) and hang lantern shade curtains.

Clean lens inside & out, lubricate mechanisms if required. Check all optic alarm systems, leaving lights and systems in "ready to run" status.

Sweep & wash lantern floor and all tower stairways/landings to base level. Dust or damp wipe all ledges and sills en route.

Pump fresh water to fill header tanks sufficient for daily use. Pump sea water to toilet header tank (if applicable).

Clean, vacuum, all domestic areas including toilet. Launder tea cloths etc.

Switch over generator engine set to next engine in rotation line. Clean last duty engine and any surplus oil around engine bed. Wash/degrease Engine Room floor space.

Check/Time Radio Beacon (if applicable), Conduct Radio Transmitter test with other stations within group; test to include 21.82khz and group working frequency. On VHF test Channel 16 & TH private channel.

LEAVE ALL NAVIGATION /COMMUNICATION SYSTEMS IN READY STATUS.

Daily: Duty cook to clean cooker/Rayburn/kitchen on completion of meals.

In addition to above

MONDAY:

Clean all station brightwork including Engine Room. Polish brass/copperwork.

TUESDAY:

Clean outside Lantern glazing and tower window exteriors (weather conditions permitting)

WEDNESDAY :

Check all station batteries. Check cells with hydrometer and record readings in battery log (duplicate). Clean and regrease all battery tops. Wash battery rackings, ledges etc, including floor space.

THURSDAY:

Test Fog Signal for min ten minutes duration on each of all compressor sets. On completion, ensure air storage tanks contain minimum of air required to commence sounding. Ensure all plant left in clean order and all systems in ready status.

FRIDAY:

Clean all inside glazing and tower windows. Regrease hinge pins and window bolts as necessary.

## SATURDAY:

Check/dip all fuel tanks. Check water tank levels, bottled gas and coal /anthracite stocks. Record all readings and transmit stock figures to Group coordinating station or direct to TH as appropriate.

## SUNDAY:

Wind all station clocks. Any other duties as designated by Principal Keeper.

## ADDITIONAL PRE RELIEF DUTIES TO INCLUDE:

Safety cleaning of all landings (lime wash).

All engines to receive oil change, filter clean/change, injectors checked/ changed.

All bunks to be disinfectant washed immediately pre relief.

Emergency rations, First Aid cabinet and dangerous drug stock check. Record and reorder stocks as necessary.

Explosives/flares/distress rockets to be checked as in good usable status.

Helipad to be cleaned of bird debris and checked as in non slip condition.

Hand held "walkie talkie" radios to be checked /charged ready for use.

## RELIEF DAY (HELICOPTER RELIEF STATIONS)

## MORNING WATCH:

Duty Keeper to send full meteorology weather report to Helicopter Ops.

Visual check of helipad area including safety netting etc.

All helicopter safety equipment & Fire Extinguishers to be placed in position on helideck.

GENERAL:

Test radio calls to be made on aviation working frequency and radio to be close monitored throughout flying operations.

Ensure that all freight for transit is weighed, labelled, and load sheet completed for Flight Engineer attention. Inform Heli ops prior to commencement of operations.

Keeper remaining on station, or other appointed person to assume role of Heli Deck Fire Attendant (wearing high visibility, Fire protective suit)

Any other duties as designated by Principal Keeper.

RELIEF DAY (BOAT RELIEF STATIONS)

MORNING WATCH:

Duty Keeper to send full present weather & landing state report to Boatman/Trinity House Depot/ Trinity House Vessel Commander, as applicable.

Further landing /weather condition updates to be forwarded noting any deterioration/improvement of situation around station.

Landing gear/cranes /mooring chains to be rigged and lifebuoys etc to be put in position if probable potential for relief.

As can be noted from the Daily Routine orders, much of the Lighthouse Keepers time was taken in carrying out, what could best be described as, "household tasks," such good house keeping practices being essential in maintaining what was both a Lighthouse and "home" for the duty period. Most such tasks, are self explanatory, but, others, whilst seemingly routine, deserve further explanation; one such being that of cleaning outside glazing! This term could be used to describe "window cleaning," except that within the context of a lighthouse, it takes call for a slightly different approach. It was particularly important that the lantern glazing was kept scrupulously clean in order to ensure the best possible output from the main navigation light; with almost constant sea spray and "calling cards" being left by sea birds, this was no simple task!

The lantern area of almost all lighthouses is made up of diamond shaped, slightly curved, panels of glass, in some cases, almost half inch in thickness; the only way of cleaning being from a ladder. Not for the squeamish! Such work could only safely be undertaken during periods of low wind speed, even then, demanding the utmost of care.

Whilst wearing a safety harness, itself clipped into links provided around the glazing area circumference, the "window cleaner" ascended a ladder which was hooked into a rail at gutter level, thus preventing it from falling backwards. With all possible precautions having been taken, the only other requirement, (mine anyway!), was not to look down! Personally, whilst always taking my duty turn in glazing cleaning, I have to admit to this task was my least favourite of all Lighthouse Routine orders, and I always felt quietly pleased on its' completion. With the exception of a few, in my experience, most of my fellow Keepers felt much as I did regarding this particular aspect of our work. As a task, it was essential, but as hobby, NO! It might come as a surprise to some to learn that, whilst the height aspect of lighthouses did not really bother me too much, cleaning my own gutters at home did!

The majority of lighthouses maintained an output power of at least one million candela, each having a range of between 20-27 miles, all of which could be easily reduced by obscured glazing. A team of TH

Engineers regularly checked the effective "light ranges" of all lights on a regular basis, from which findings, any increases or otherwise necessary to output power (ie bulb wattage etc), could be met.

During periods of blizzard snow, it was necessary for the Keepers to try and prevent snow blown against the lantern from freezing on the ice cold glass, and I recall how, on one occasion, the wind and blizzard conditions were just too severe to even venture outside on to the gallery. (Needles 1978). We were helpless against it, and had no alternative but to rely upon the Fog Signal to assist our reduced lighting output, and in the following daylight, the storm having passed, our having to scrape what had become sheet ice from around the lantern surrounds.

On occasions, glazing panels were in need of replacement, this task being part of a Mechanics' remit. The panels were held in position by strips of gun metal, bolted into the main lantern framework, and bedded in a mastic seal for additional weatherproofing. Gun metal was in extensive use in a, particularly Rock Tower, Lighthouse structure; it did not corrode, was tough, yet reasonably easily adjusted or maintained on site as part of a full mechanical, usually annual, service. Main doors, all framings, and exterior step rungs, (known as "Dog Steps"), are to be found in Bishop Rock, Eddystone, Longships, and Wolf Rock, to name a few examples of well known stations.

When stationed offshore on a Tower Lighthouse, the question of how to keep fit posed certain difficulties; this being a particular problem during times of severe weather. In summer it was often possible to get outside and "stroll" the landing area, and, if desired, to even jog in an effort to attain some degree of fitness. Enjoying good meals as we did, does little for the figure unless, at least some of those calories are used up!

The first, and perhaps most obvious, form of exercise came purely by nature of the building itself; that being that almost everything needed was either up or down some very steep stairways! Step aerobics practiced, at no expense, by simply just carrying out normal keeper duties, the drawback to which was, having done so for a month or two using stairs, which, in some cases were little more than step ladders, the backs of ones' knees would ache quite considerably when at first ashore on leave, and walking on the level. We came to know each and every stair on a personal basis!

I recall how, on the Wolf Rock, we kept a rowing machine up in the lantern; this proved to a major asset, and, with which, as a matter of light hearted, competitive pride, we each tried to increase our rowing speeds and times, our fitness improving as stamina levels built up.

After two a half years as a Supernumerary Assistant, I at last received word that I was to be promoted ("made up" in grapevine speak!), to Assistant Keeper; this meant having a station appointment of my own. I was undertaking relief duty at Needles when the "Lighthouse grapevine" news came in over the radio; having, on so many previous occasions heard the promotions and transfers list come in, I was elated at finding my own name on it!

The "grapevine" information was that I was to be appointed to Lynmouth Foreland Lighthouse (N.Devon), my elation was coupled with a mixture of disbelief, and I could not wait to tell my wife and family. Next day brought more "grapevine news" that I was to be appointed to Nab Tower! It was only when at home on leave some two weeks later, that I received the formal letter appointing me to Needles Lighthouse! I was to take up duty at my new appointment following a short spell at Bishop Rock (Scillies). Having previously served on several occasions at Needles, I was more than pleased with the news, and with my home leave coinciding with Christmas, I really felt that my cake was well iced!

Having a station appointment meant an end to all the uncertainties associated with life as a "Super," not least in knowing, within reason, just when, one would be home or away on a month on/off cycle. Just a glance at the calender would inform all as to whether I would be around for a family birthday, Christmas etc. Pencilled rings around calender dates provided a kind of settled lifestyle when compared to the previous two and half years! Month on and off involved taking all family events as they arrived, this, quite naturally, included Christmas, a time when everyone would really rather be at home; however, the compensation came in being able to enjoy six months holiday every year! When others were working in their civilian roles, the Lighthouse Keeper was enjoying several weeks off at a stretch, and all those household tasks such as decorating etc, were easily dealt with!

My SAK time had been valuable to me, both in gaining the best experience of different stations, and in having the opportunity of meeting and serving with so many other Lighthouse Keepers, each themselves having interesting stories to tell of their own service lives and times. It was always of interest to me that, on arrival at a new station for relieving duties, the serving Keepers were always keen to hear of any news regarding my previously visited Lighthouses, and to enquire about their colleagues. The SAK was often the best source of the latest news and much more personal than the "grapevine!" Visiting maintenance personnel were another welcome source of information, with, in their case, the additional benefit of their base, Blackwall being close to Trinity House, London, they often possessed Headquarters news following meetings of the Board.

During my SAK service, I served at eleven different Lighthouses, both Rock and Land Stations, often returning to some on numerous relief duty occasions.

During my early career, all promotions relied upon "dead mans' shoes" in order to progress the promotion ladder; this did not wholly require a death (Thank the Lord!), a simple retirement of a Keeper was quite sufficient! I had, during my SAK service, arrived at a time when there were a number of younger age group Keepers, this fact leading to a period of slower promotions. Some years following however, the promotion system was altered to become a merit, rather than age, system, this to we younger men, was a great encouragement.

My family had been most supportive of me throughout my SAK service, but, like me, were quite delighted at moving on to the next, and long awaited, career step! I was particularly pleased at being appointed to a Rock station ,as, having our own house, we would not be compelled to move to Trinity House accommodation as would have been the case with a Land Station posting. Being in our own property made us eligible for the welcome payment of House Allowance, paid in lieu of not being in Service housing!

# SECTION TWO
# REAL LIGHTHOUSE KEEPING, BISHOP
# ROCK, AND OTHERS

The Rocks, as they were typically known were graded into three catagories according to isolation, confinement and amenity etc. Class One accounted for the tower or pillar stations, Lights such as Bishop Rock, Needles, Eddystone and others are good such examples, with Class two referring to stations on uninhabited islands, which, whilst still isolated, afford a certain amount of exercise space and living spaces are better appointed; Lighthouses in this catagory include, Flatholm (Bristol Chan.), Round Is (Scillies), and Casquets (Chan Is.), Lastly, class three stations cover lighthouses such as Lundy (Bristol Chan), Alderney (Channel Is), and Sark (Channel Is).In this third group, Keepers are living as on any other rock station but could take advantage of nearby shops and facilities. Payment of "Rock Allowance" was awarded for each day on station,or standing by for relief to such station; premium rate being paid for class one, and scaled down through the remaining classifications.

Class one towers carried a time limit posting duration whereupon an appointed Keeper could request a transfer without having to give any reason; Wolf Rock, was one such station on which two years was deemed to be the limit of service. These rulings were particularly appropriate when all reliefs were via boat, and long overdue periods were commonplace; the advent of helicopter useage relaxed the real need for time limited service, although it was still accepted that too much "tower time" was not good for any one individual for prolonged periods of service. On some stations, with the interior stairways being little more than step ladder style, and fresh air being much restricted, questions of risks to health were raised by some. Trinity House ensured that all Keepers underwent a full chest X-Ray every three years during their service, all fees being paid by the Authority.

On finding out that I was a Lighthouse Keeper, many questions were asked of me, as was explained, "we've never ever met a real Lighthouse Keeper before!" There seemed some wonderment and curiousity, that men could ever isolate themselves for many weeks or months at a time, away from mankind, their families included. I felt perhaps, that they felt us to be a little eccentric or strange in some way, as, "they couldn't possibly ever do that!" This perception, I found mildly amusing especially when friends who knew me well expressed it! I have always enjoyed the company of others; this knowledge, I feel, is what added to their amazement! "What made you want to be a Lighthouse Keeper?" "Are you married?" "What does your wife feel about it?" and finally, the favourite and most used question of, "Isn't it Boring?" All these questions and more are perfectly valid, and I have always tried to fully explain to the enquirer, just what it is like, and just what advantages it afforded, not just myself, but the wider family also. With that, some even expressed envy at my situation!

In an isolated off shore lighthouse, its' crew are its' driving force; without whom no power could be generated, no daily maintenance undertaken, and ultimately no reliable functioning navigation aids for the Mariner. These basic requirements plus the Keepers watchful eyes dictate the need for well ordered processes and routines to be followed to the letter. Effective crew tasking, from the stations' Principal Keeper and his two Assistants ensure that all such routines are effectively carried out, with each man knowing both his own job and and that of his colleagues. In the event of a crew member being taken sick and off duty, the workload can be, and is, reliably continued, and the very highest of TH standards and services to the Mariner upheld. Somewhere, in the midst of this well ordered routine of operation, there exists the interference of "Murphys' Law!" introducing, perhaps, a generator failure, main lamp malfunction, or any one of a number of problems which fall within the "sent to try us" category! Thanks to good teamwork and pooled experience, no problem proved unable to resolve. With our daily tasks complete, domestic work included, the Lighthouse Keeper could relax and follow his own interests, be that, a good book, music , or a host of other hobbies; the lighthouse was rich in "me time!"

As I had previously discovered at Longships, the Rock Lighthouse tower is purely functional and, by nature, dedicated to the effectiveness of its' navigational aids with little space for its inhabitants, the Keepers. Life within the the Tower mean living with the constant drone of the generators and their associated fumes, which, despite high power extractor fans, were difficult to entirely eliminate, especially during winter, when high seas rendered extraction largely ineffective.

Life for the Tower Lighthouse Keeper, often meant having to endure, sometimes for several days and nights, the continuous moan of the air driven Fog Horn, as it sent out it's mournful warning in times of poor visibility. During such conditions, restful sleep becomes virtually impossible and, as I learned, drastic measures were undertaken by some to resolve the problem. I remember one Blackwall Mechanic (name withheld!), who , swore by a "swig" of cough linctus from the medical cabinet to ensure undisturbed sleep in times of fog. It was much later in my service, that I learned on reading the label, that the mixture contained Morphine; peaceful sleep indeed!   Others of us would attempt to  sleep whilst wearing ear defenders ( head phones ) only to wake up with a start after turning over and almost amputating an ear! It was always a welcome relief when the fog cleared and (quiet) normality returned. Conversations during fog sounding were punctuated by the blast, obviously causing frequent interruption, in some cases, for ten seconds every one minute; this made it quite difficult to enjoy normal chat, the fog horn having been shut down.   All lighthouses both on and off shore, have fog signals as part of their navigation aid warning systems; on a tower the fog emitters, and, in some cases, the engines also, are on a floor immediately above the bedroom.

The most unnerving experience of all to any new Lighthouse keeper was to be in  tower rock lighthouse during a storm; my first such experience was when undertaking my first ever rock duty at Longships lighthouse. I should have realised that, being January, such bad weather is purely a seasonal event and should certainly not have been unexpected! The sea rolls in with a relentless deepening swell, this massive weight of water hitting the tower with an awesome crash, before climbing higher up the structure, often rolling its' way to the very top. The tower quivers and shakes violently, whilst strange, loud, almost metallic sounds, reverberate through the structure, seemingly coming from the very depths of the rock itself. As the water recedes back down the tower, it sucks the very air from within via the window scupper vents; water hits glass as if it isn't water at all, but something much more solid. Hard to comprehend just how such a substance as soft as water can carry with it so much power and weight. Under these circumstances, the outer shutters are rammed closed, this creates a continuation of the smooth, almost clarinet shape, of the tower exterior walls; on the inside of the several feet thickness of the walls, the windows are closed and locked with a screw in fastening making the lighthouse as weatherproof as is possible. In the severest of weather, some seepage of water is inevitable, and calls for the use of the bucket and mop at frequent intervals!

A rock tower kitchen sink, also had a uniqueness to it, in that during bad weather, a spout of pressured water would periodically erupt from the plug hole! The reason for this geyser like attraction was that the lead waste outlet pipe, part of the original construction, came out through the granite wall at a point almost down at sea level; as the sea rolled in, some would inevitably force its' way in and up the pipe! Under the sink, as part of the waste outlet, Trinity House plumbers had installed a valve, which, after using the sink, would need to be secured in the closed position to prevent waterspouts; fine until dishwater on the way down, met high pressure sea water coming up! Not a pleasant result! station and it,s crew,to whom everyday was very much the same as any other in daily operations.On a personal note,however,we each had our own ways of marking the changes from days into weeks, as our month,(or two),of duty turn progressed.

No matter how one tried, there were only so many different meal recipes available to the lighthouse keeper, the main constraint being lack of fresh, available ingredients, and also the lack of storage facility available within deep freezers shared by the station complement. Meals, particularly lunches, were relatively easy, and enjoyed by all; we almost always had a roast lunch several times weekly,and at other times perhaps a curry or freshly caught (summer only) fish or shellfish. Fresh vegetables were usually stored in the cold of the tower window ledges,often three feet or more thick; at best,most vegetables, potatoes excepted, would only stay usable for a couple of weeks maximum,,after which,in pre freezer days,,it was all down to tins!

Tea times, however, seemed to most, to pose the greatest difficulty in varying the menu; one can only have so many boiled egg or cheese sandwiches, and/or tins of fruit before monotony begins to set in! It was only when at home discussing this very subject with my wife that a solution was offered; why not ,every Sunday, make a rule for yourself by having something completely different! Like what? And so, the Sunday jelly was instigated! Every Saturday evening I would mix up a jelly and rest in the fridge to await my Sunday high tea, it was such a simple idea; on my store shelf stood four jellies for every months duty, when jelly number four disappeared it was then time for me to go as well!

One whole made up jelly is rather a lot for just one person,even with my appetite, and so,with time, one by one my fellow keepers joined in, one with a tin of fruit to add to the jelly,and much later,the other with a can of processed cream. High tea on a Lighthouse Sunday was now fully established as a shared effort and looked forward to by all on station.1 continued my jelly tradition all throughout my subsequent years of service, and irrespective of whatever station I was a part .The half way mark of a duty turn was "cake day".Having brought with me, a cake from home, this was a "bit of home" shared as a special treat to mark the start of our downhill run towards relief day!

During my earlier years in the service,I have to confess to being a smoker*, as, indeed seemingly, most of us in the lighthouse were,it was essential, therefore to ensure that enough tobacco etc was packed for the trip. In order to break the monotony of "rolled cigarettes", and to assist in the Sunday jelly commemorations, every weekend I would open a packet of 20 "tailor made" cigarettes to enjoy by way of a change, whilst at same time contributing to the marking of my duty time.Five packs of tipped cigarettes equalled one packet to be opened each weekend, usually Saturdays, and the fifth pack to be enjoyed on relief day itself;arguably the most nerve teasing day of one's whole turn, a day filled with many questions as to whether or not we would be able to get off the lighthouse.Once sat in the helicopter or boat, big sighs of relief (no pun intended !),and,in the case of the boat, ,another fagl This time in celebration of being homeward bound!We each seemed to have our own, private ways of dealing with the ordered monotony of routine; in addition to the more outward and obvious ways listed above, others would perhaps have that special phone call (phones were a much later addition),or with some ito uld be listening to a particular radio programme which they knew would be listened to by those at home.

The Bishop Rock Lighthouse, in the Isles of Scilly, Trinity House's tallest tower lighthouse, was built in 1853,but, owing to high seas frequently obscuring the light, the tower was strengthened, and it's height increased, some years later. The following text is of the original commemorative plaques which remain on the Bishop to record the achievement ;

THIS TOWER WAS ERECTED BY THE CORPORATION OF TRINITY HOUSE OF DEPTFORD STROUD, LONDON. THE FIRST STONE, ONE OF THE FIFTH COURSE, WAS LAID ON THE 14th JULY 1852 IN THE 16th YEAR OF THE REIGN OF HER MAJESTY QUEEN VICTORIA. HIS GRACE, THE DUKE OF WELLINGTON, MASTER. CAPTAIN SIR JOHN HENRY POLLY, B.I. DEPUTY MASTER.

THE LOWEST STONE WAS AFTERWARDS LAID IN A CHASM OF ROCK AT ONE FOOT BELOW THE LEVEL OF LOW WATER SPRING TIDES ON THE 30th JULY 1852. THE

STONEWORK OF THE TOWER WAS FINISHED ON THE 28th AUGUST 1857.

THE LIGHT WAS FIRST EXHIBITED ON THE 1st SEPT.1858. HIS ROYAL HIGHNESS, THE PRINCE CONSORT, MASTER,AND CAPTAIN JOHN SHEPHERD, DEPUTY MASTER. THE SUCCESSFUL TERMINATION OF THIS MOST DIFFICULT UNDERTAKING WAS ACCOMPLISHED WITHOUT LOSS OF LIFE, OR SERIOUS ACCIDENT TO ANY PERSON EMPLOYED. " DEO SOLI GLORIA"

JAMES WALKER, ENGINEER.
NICHOLAS DOUGLASS, SUPERINTENDENT.

The 2nd Plaque reads:

THE CYLINDRICAL BASE AT THE FOOT OF THIS TOWER, THE OUTER WALL, AND THE THREE UPPER CHAMBERS, AND LANTERN, WERE UNDERTAKEN BY THE CORPORATION OF TRINITY HOUSE, IN ORDER TO OBTAIN INCREASED HEIGHT FOR THE LIGHT, AND GIVE INCREASED STABILITY TO THE STRUCTURE.THE FIRST STONE WAS LAID ON 21st MAY 1883, H.R.H. THE DUKE OF EDINBURGH, K.G.MASTER, ADMIRAL SIR RICHARD COLLINSON K.C.B, DEPUTY MASTER. THE STONEWORK WAS COMPLETED ON THE 3rd SEPTEMBER 1886.THE IMPROVED LIGHT WAS EXHIBITED FIRST TEMPORARILY ON THE 25th MAY 1886 AND FROM THE HYPER RADIAL APPARATUS ON THE 25 th OCTOBER 1887 IN THE REIGN OF HER MAJESTY QUEEN VICTORIA.

ADMIRAL H.R.H. THE DUKE OF EDINBURGH ,MASTER, CAPTAIN JOHN SIDNEY WEBB, DEPUTY MASTER.THIS ADDITIONAL UNDERTAKING WAS SCARCELY LESS

DIFFICULT THAN THE FIRSTHAND WAS MARKED BY A CONTINUANCE OF IMMUNITY FROM ACCIDENT AS MARKED ABOVE; " UNTO THEE O LORD DO WE GIVE THANKS"

## SIR JAMES NICHOLAS DOUGLASS, E in C WILLIAM TREGARTHEN DOUGLASS, RESIDENT ENGINEER.

The Bishop Rock is a true marvel of Civil Engineering, being built of granite, in the beautifully formed shape reminiscent of an upturned clarinet. It is this very shaping that offers least resistance to the sea, allowing the swell to roll up the tower, dissipating it's force as it climbs. From inside the tower one can observe how, at the higher levels, the walls are some 3 feet in thickness, gradually increasing to some 8-9 feet at the base, each individual stone being dovetailed, woodwork fashion, into the next. These Rock towers, are, themselves, an experience, not least in increasing one's own respect for the sea and it's power, versus Man's ingenuity and skill, mostly applied using pure manpower skills, applied without the aid of such technology and machinery that we often take for granted today. Each stone was meticulously shaped and sculpted by hand from rough, hard granite, by Masons having little, except hammers, chisels, and a great deal of craftsmanship.Rock tower Lt Houses were all constructed over a century ago, and it is to both the Engineers who designed and built them, and to the regular structural maintenance applied to them by Trinity House, that full credit is duly deserved; for, throughout their history, with most lighthouses having been constructed during Victorian times, they have stood like solitary sentries, defying the power of raw nature itself. Each winter, on the Western Rock stations, ( Wolf Rock, Longships, and Bishop Rock) sections of the rooftop heli-decks are either damaged, or disappear completely, as a result of storms and associated seas, and, on occasions, some areas of lantern glazing has also suffered damage.Inside a tall tower, battened down against the storm, Keepers just "got on with their job," the severe weather outside posing more of an inconvenience than anything else! During daylight hours, the closed storm shutters prevented any real daylight from entering the building, with the associated lack of fresh air soon becoming apparent. Cooking, mainly by solid fuel or oil fired Rayburn type stove, became a challenge as upward draught necessary for good burning, became intercepted by high seas at the top! Meals, in such situations, were either very early, or simply just "delayed!" For the television fans, the seas caused great disruption, whenever the seas reached the top of the lighthouse the television signal was interrupted, usually at the critical point in the film; more than once, finding out "whodunit" had to wait for the repeat episode! It was not uncommon for the entire television arial to go "walkabout" never to be seen again; rock tower lighthouses always needed to ensure that a spare arial or two, were in the stores ready!

I arrived at Bishop Rock Lighthouse via helicopter; it was the period now referred to as "twixt mas," which, having been fortunate in spending the main festive season at home, I would now be on board the light for New Year. This, I did not mind in the least, I was still revelling in the fact that, following my Bishop tour, I would be taking up my promotion and appointment at Needles. Helicopter relief to Bishop had been somewhat different to my previous trip there which was in the old traditional way via boat. Viewing the Bishop Rock from seaward at the tower base was quite a moving experience, the lighthouse ,at 47 metres in height is awesome in its' might, and a long way up when on the end of a rope! Having tied a bow line loop in the rope, then inserted one foot(the other gripping the line) and maintaining a tight hold, fellow keepers would winch you up whilst the Boatman kept tension on the back line, thus preventing body slams into the tower! It was quite an experience, rare even then , with relief by air the regular method. The Bishop had, for many years, but particularly during the 1920's and 30's, served as the English marker for the Blue Riband trophy which was awarded for the fastest transatlantic crossing, the American marker being the Ambrose Lightvessel. The winning of this award was much coveted, and eagerly contested by transatlantic liners of all flags; more recently, during the 1980's, it was challenged by Sir Richard Branson in his vessel, Virgin Atlantic Challenger.

*BISHOP ROCK RELIEF BY BOAT, NOT FOR THE FAINT HEARTED!*

Serving on Bishop were two long serving Keepers, Andy (PK), and Russ (AK), both of whom resided in the Trinity House cottages at St Marys' on Scillies. Whilst Russ was the quieter one and liked nothing more than watching TV, Andy was a mild eccentric and a laugh a minute. Andy was a radio "ham" (G3 UUZ I think!!) and soon after our arrival on station was busy rigging up his antenna and testing his radio gear in readiness for use during our turn.I spent many a happy hour down in the kitchen listening to Andy as he transmitted, literally worldwide from a lonely lighthouse! As the Bishop had three amenity rooms as opposed to most stations two, Andys' radio could not be heard by anyone trying to enjoy television which was two floors above in the lounge; the bedroom being the room in between.

One recollection of my Bishop Rock service with Andy and Russ is an amusing, yet a trifle embarrassing moment for Russ, whose dear lady had prepared, and frozen, a selection of delightful pies, some steak, and others of blackberry and apple. Myself being cook of the day,I had prepared a roast with all the trimmings, and Russ had duly presented me with a steak pie as his meat choice. We all sat down with our roast potatoes, veg etc, and all was going well until Russ put his knife through his pie! You've guessed it! Wrong pie! My culinary delight became accompanied by blackberry and apple! Poor Russ, he had obviously gone to the wrong bag of frozen pies; in his defence, I must add that, outwardly, they were identical, sorry Russ, but they were all labeled and in two separate bags!

New Years Eve came and went during which Andy produced a bottle of fine wine for our mutual toast, whilst over the airways , we exchanged greetings with other lighthouses within our group. Leaving Bishop, all my thoughts were on transferring to Needles, whilst wondering whether ever I might possibly return to Bishop later in my career. I in fact did, but not quite under the circumstances that I had envisaged.

There is, however, one incident, concerning the Bishop Rock, appropriate to record at this point, which well illustrates the need to guard against complacency regarding the might of the sea, versus a man-made, structure. Upon completion of automation work by Trinity House engineers, the last keepers left the Bishop Rock, at Xmas 1993, since which time the station has been controlled and monitored, via computer link, by Trinity House, at Harwich, from where, in February 1994, a report was received that a Fire Alarm was effective out on the Lt Hse. A team from Lizard Lighthouse, with myself included, accompanied by a Fire Officer and Trinity House Electrician, flew out to investigate and assess the problem; upon arrival, we discovered no fire, but in the Base of the tower, a scene of absolute devastation.

One of a pair of metal doors, each of which weighing some half a ton, had been completely stove in, and was lying on the floor, the other hung, twisted and buckled, on it's only remaining hinge mounting. The full force of the sea had, for the only time since it's construction, entered the building and destroyed all fittings, the shower installation, fridge and deep freeze, and all else in it's path. It was a sight defiant of all belief, and destroyed all my previous ideas of a lighthouse tower's impregnability.

Following our immediate status report, a maintenance team was dispatched from Trinity House, Penzance. Their task was to ensure the safety of the lighthouse tower which they did using steel shuttering with which to secure the doorway and keep out any ingress by seas; it was fortunate that local weather was relatively calm, but being February, sea conditions could change at any time. New replacement doors, exact replicas of the originals were cast and hung the following Spring/ Summer, this in itself, was a major task calling for mechanics to be suspended from outside the tower in order to fit the doors from the exterior, not for the squeamish!

There have been several differing theories as to why, after having well stood the test of time, these tower doors, gave way. One such theory, perhaps a little far fetched, which expounds the fact that for almost a week prior to the incident, severe gales had been blowing from the South East (this is in direct line to the doorway). The tower having stood for over one hundred years, it would have experienced more than its share of gales from all directions ,so nothing of any real note there!

This gale, however, was different in that a large freighter hd sank in the Atlantic shedding its deck cargo of bulk timber much of which found its way on to the Scilly Isles and the delighted residents! On the day that we flew out to investigate the alarm call, we flew over rocky islets strewn with large bulks of timber; on the beaches of the larger islands, locals with tractors were eagerly dragging their finds up on to dry land. Some such timber, had, we later learned, found its way on to the beaches of West Cornwall, some thirty miles distant.

It has been suggested, that, such large pieces of timber, much of which was mahogany, might well have crashed against the main doors of the Bishop tower, acting as a battering ram, ultimately weakening them sufficiently for the force of the sea to complete the task, and allow its ingress into the structure. Co-incidental ? maybe; but impossible, no !

It defies imagination as to just how it would have felt to have been inside that Lt House during this incident, with all it's associated noise of, not only the sea, but of the sound of breakages within. One would probably seriously have believed that the end had come. The base of the Lighthouse is sealed off by a, bolted down, metal hatch which isolates the lower room from others, in case of fuel leakages from the tanks above. Although found badly buckled, it is probably this hatch which confined the damage to just the base, therefore protecting the main structural masonry; the tower relying on it's exterior shape for it's protection, not having been designed against attack from the inside. The reason for the Fire Alarm ? Salt water causing a short-circuit in the base level fire detection sensor !

As a foot-note to this unfortunate incident at the Bishop Rock Lighthouse, 1 think that all of us, whilst still feeling safe and secure when on station, then possessed a realisation that, despite lighthouse structures having been well tried and tested by nature at it's most ferocious, there  always remains the thought that it is only man made, and should never be taken for granted. It is hoped that, in the near future, the damaged ex-Bishop doors will be displayed in a National

Lighthouse Museum , to enable all to see, at first hand, just what force an angry sea can command.

In conclusion, and on a lighter note, I feel that the following theory offered by a colleague and wit is worthy of mention; that being, that nothing like this ever before occurred until someone decided to put a cat-flap in the door ! There's no real answer to that is there ?

Our visit to Bishop Rock, on that occasion, formed part of duties performed much later in my career, whilst stationed at Lizard Lighthouse, Cornwall, by which time, many stations had been automated and their Keepers withdrawn. I chose to include  the episode of the severe storm as ,to me, it felt appropriate to the Bishop Rock and its' long and distinguished history. Further information regarding the automation programme is included in later pages, and so to return to March 1978 and my new appointment to Needles Lighthouse, Isle of Wight !

My permanent appointment to Needles was not my first ever visit there, as mentioned earlier, it was whilst serving on that very Lighthouse that I received, via "grapevine news," information regarding my promotion.1976 saw a "heatwave"  summer, with temperatures in the mid 70's for several months; I was fortunate to have served at Needles through July and August of that year; the sea was a picture postcard ,flat calm shade of blue, and remained so right throughout our entire duty turn. Never once did we close the tower door or any of the windows! It was at Needles that I met up with Principal Keeper Brian H, and was he who, with his  great sense of humour, and outlook on Lighthouse life, made my stay just perfect! Our relief was by local boat from Yarmouth, Isle of Wight, and it was there that Brians' wife dropped him off with all his provisions etc; as we sailed down the calm Solent in the sun, heading for Needles, Brian outlined the "plan"for the duty turn! He described it as x amount of One Day cricket Internationals, so many Gillette Cup matches, a few other games, and then we would be home again! Clearly,as I was to learn, a keen sportsman! He also me that, during the "turn," Brians wife would be delivering fresh vegetables and salad ingredients, to the Boatmans' house, all fresh from their garden at home on the Island! This would find its way out to us in due course on his "Trips around the Needles" tourist run! Everything that Brian had said would happen, DID!

I was a little disappointed to find that, on my appointment to Needles, I would be serving on the "opposite turn" to Brian, who did, however, shortly following my arrival, be transferred down West! Many years later, we were to meet up again.

The Needles, as a posting was a very good station, it was a cut above that of the average Tower Rock Lighthouse, in that we did not suffer the extreme conditions endured further west. In addition, the Needles afforded a sense of community amongst the Isle of Wight locals, not least, in summer, when pleasure craft of all descriptions would be all around us and our own regular Boatman, Tony, would call in with, and collect, mail, as he conducted his "trips around the Needles" from nearby Alum Bay. Our mail was collected and delivered with amazing regularity, even to the luxury of first and second class mail! The visitors in the boat seemed to enjoyed meeting us, and we them; almost everyday, someone would kindly donate a newspaper, all this on a supposedly isolated offshore lighthouse!

During winter, on most Sundays, The Yarmouth Lifeboat, whilst on routine exercise, would deliver us a newspaper; when conditions were too dangerous to get in close, a rocket line was fired, to which was attached a watertight tube containing the papers!

Inside, the Needles tower was "fatter" than its' counterparts down on on the Western Rocks; we still only had the use of two main rooms for amenity use, i.e. Bedroom and Kitchen, but, all areas were much more spacious, the kitchen for example, accommodated three armchairs, in addition to a large table and dining associated chairs.

The engine room was situated at ground floor level which helped to, at least minimise noise levels, and keep the storeroom immediately above, ambiently warm with the extractor trunking and pipe work passing through it. Hanging washing in this room ensured rapid drying results! In most rock towers, there was a room specifically given over to fuel tanks; at Needles, all such fuel was stored in a man made cave within the adjacent "needle rock." This cave had originally been carved out of the chalk rock as home to the lighthouse builders, and evidence of their bunk ledges could still be found. The cave itself extended to a depth of approx 10 metres with a width of 3; ample space within which to site large fuel tanks, the supply pipework extending across the landing under iron covering against the elements. Our cave also housed our main coal bunker, from which we topped up an internal store when weather permitted.

*NEEDLES LIGHTHOUSE 1978*

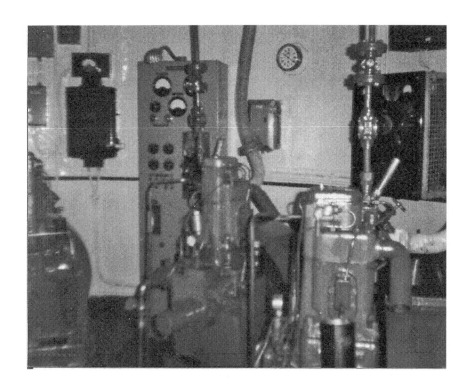

*NEEDLES LIGHTHOUSE ENGINE ROOM*

Winter cooking and heating was supplied by a solid fuel Rayburn range,the chimney of which provided surprisingly good warmth right throughout the tower above. In common with all other such lighthouses, the coffee pot simmered at all times, and a very large kettle ensured that hot water was available whenever needed. Our Rayburn offered the best toaster in the world! Opening the door to a glowing bed of anthracite, and with a slice of bread on the toasting fork, seemingly within seconds, a round of toast, second to none, was ready for its' butter! From my fellow Keepers,I learnt that a "chunky" portion of bacon impaled on the fork, provided a well cooked , crispy delight delivered quicker (and tastier!),than any microwave could ever provide! I soon made sure that "bacon misshapes" formed part of any winter food order; apparently, cooking this way was the practice of train drivers in the age of steam railways!

We endured many a period when the tower was battered by severe weather and high seas, but, in my experience, it was seldom as bad or as prolonged, as that of other more exposed tower rock lighthouses such as Bishop or Longships; we were, after all, tucked under the Isle of Wight which effectively blocked wind from certain directions, particularly from "Easterlies." Gales from the South West, however, found us the target of huge, rolling swells, which, long after the demise of the gale, continued often for several days before finally quietening down. It was during such weather, particularly when our relief date was drawing closer, that, I could not help but question as to why I was serving on the only Rock station in the service that was still reliant on a boat!

I recall how on relief day, on awaking, my first thoughts were as to the sea state and listening for the sea, and the thumping sound that it made as it hit the tower. Experience soon taught me how to assess by ear, the relief prospects for that day; the answer came by counting the time between the waves thump and the sound of splashing, broken water. A time duration of more than some eight seconds usually signified despair, particularly if the noise was coming from the south west side of the building! However, despite disappointment on the day, once the weather improved, and we were in the boat en route towards shore, all was soon well, in the knowledge that we were on our way home, duty turn completed, and nothing else mattered!

The Rock Lighthouse Keepers working routine of month on and off, as the envy of many friends at home. They saw it as a kind of Utopia when compared to their own annual leave entitlement of just a few weeks off per year; what they tended to overlook was that our duties continued throughout the whole year round, not ceasing because it was Christmas or some other long established Bank Holiday. Our month duty periods was the only way in which, we Keepers could enjoy anything close to the 40 hour week enjoyed by most of the working population in so called, "normal jobs." It had been initiated by the publication of a Government White Paper enquiry into Lighthouse Keepers hours and conditions, and not something ever requested by Lighthouse or Lightvessel crews.

Many Lighthouse personnel had actually opposed it as they felt that, in terms of allowances paid when offshore, they would lose financially!

The duty month away from home, and in virtual isolation from the social world, proved too much to bear for some, especially amongst newer entrants; no Friday night darts, and little chance to celebrate family occasions, i.e. Anniversaries, Birthdays etc. Indeed, nothing on a truly regular basis as enjoyed by those in "civvy street." Such difficulties also equally affected families at home, with some family relationships suffering immense strain as a result; this stress, on some occasions, resulted in resignations from the service. It is to the detriment of no one that such measures had to be taken by some, promisingly efficient Lighthouse Keepers; it has always been my personal view that life for those at home was probably more difficult for those with families, than for us out on station. No married Keeper could do his job effectively if he could not feel certain that his wife and family at home were able to cope with his absence; it is the wife and mother that, for half the year at least, (longer in SAK time), effectively became a single parent.

Whilst, in terms of Lighthouse comforts and amenities, Needles offered much in comparison with our far west counterparts, come the days of relief in winter, stations with helipads had much less to worry over than we, still relying on boats.

Our contract local boatman, Christian name Tony, knew the waters around Needles intimately, his family over many generations past, had served the Needles Lighthouse as local boatman. On one occasion, Tony showed us a photograph of his grandfather rowing out to the Lighthouse to effect a relief; considering the distance involved of several miles through very strong tides, this must surely have demanded much effort. Where reliefs were concerned, if Tony deemed conditions unfit for relief, one could be well assured that this was so, but it was almost unheard of, that once having ventured out to the lighthouse, often in atrocious conditions, Tony would not secure a successful relief. Often, almost surfing into the landing on a south westerly swell, we would, with each pass of the landing steps, we would exchange one man with his corresponding opposite number off the lighthouse and into the boat. Once personnel exchange was completed, gear and baggage was thrown up to waiting hands as the boat swept past; this whole relief operation often taking an hour or more to complete, with the boat having to "stand off" and await the next lull in breaking seas before running in again to continue the task. In these conditions, only boatmen with good local knowledge and experience could ever get near to the lighthouse landing given the inherent danger of hazardous rocks and tide rips. In addition to local conditions adjacent to the landing, consideration needed to be given as to the risk of personnel being caught unawares by any rogue swell sweeping the upper landing and lighthouse doorway. It was sometimes the case that one Keeper had to be placed at the Lighthouse door in order to forewarn anyone on the landing steps of impending high waves, giving them the best chance of taking shelter.

It was on a day of foul weather, with relief by boat being out of the question, that, whilst on the VHF telephone, breaking my sad news to my wife at home , my call was overheard by the Needles Coastguard (situated on the clifftop behind us), and an exercising Search & Rescue helicopter from Leigh on Solent (HMS Daedulus. Following a brief,"I couldn't help overhearing,but….." introduction,I was informed that the helicopter would gladly help us out by winching personnel on and off to effect our relief; they considered that any exercise involving real people, was, to them, their means of the finest training.

Following protracted signals between ourselves, the Royal Navy and Trinity House, arrangements were made for our relief to be undertaken by helicopter; but, owing to aircraft weight restrictions, only men, personal gear, and a limited amount of food stores would be permissible. All remaining stores etc would be delivered via Tonys' boat as soon as conditions permitted.

This first time Needles helicopter relief set a precedent, in that, whenever weather conditions prohibited boat relief, we were lifted off by Royal Navy helicopter. We became great friends with the aircrews, who, on occasions, would land one or two of their number to view the lighthouse and join us for a cup of tea! We, the Keepers, agreed that, whilst none of us would take it up as a hobby, being winched on or off the tower was an answer to a prayer when down at the boat landing, sea conditions prevented any possibility for boatwork.

The search and rescue helicopters were frequent visitors to our area, often conducting training exercises using the lighthouse as a platform. On several occasions, should a Needles Keeper have been suffering toothache, then one of their helicopters has ensured quick relief from pain with a lift to the dentist!

One Christmas Day, a blackboard, on which was written festive greetings, was lowered to kitchen level, the aircrew waving their personal goodwill message as they went about their exercise patrol.

The long winter nights on station became, for me, a time for hobbies,and being a relatively new Lighthouse Keeper, I felt obliged to attempt a ship in a bottle! Beginning with "spent" main navigation lamp bulbs, I soon graduated to wine bottles; I admit to feeling quite proud of my achievements, several examples of which now adorn our Lounge at home! The light bulb variety are often the subject of much interest as each bulb has in fact, seen service at Needles or other Lighthouse.

For several years, following the leglisation of Citizens Band radio in 1981, I operated a radio station from the lighthouse, and under the "handle"(CB talk!),call sign of the "Nightlighter," spent pleasant hours talking to other operators far and wide, including under certain conditions Europe and USA. It was quite surprising to find that many people had no idea that the Needles Lighthouse, was, in fact, manned, with many at first refusing to believe in my stated location.I made many friends and received many QSL cards (confirmation of contact), from both home and abroad. Amongst my contacts were Lighthouse Keepers on other stations, including several from the northern lights on Shetland and Orkney; we compared "lighthouse lives and experiences" and exchanged respective service magazines.

The coming of summer at Needles really showed the station at its' best, good fishing, mail, and much opportunity for simply enjoying the sunshine on the fairly spacious landing area. I made up a lobster pot and caught many fine crabs and lobsters, some of which supplemented our menu, and some to take home.All this fresh air and healthy exercise, made Needles an excellent station on which to serve.

Seawards, many of the best known ocean liners passed our way at frequent intervals, such ships as QE2 and Oriana made splendid sights, especially when illuminated, as they slipped graciously past, almost in silence. By contrast, some of their cargo carrying counterparts could be heard, engines thumping noisily, from many miles away. With the port of Southampton being "just up the road," there was always much to interest the ship spotter, and we regularly received the shipping movements list in order to follow the traffic past our station.

An offshore Lighthouse was, in many respects, a self contained unit ;it's very location and difficulty of access require all who both work, and live aboard to be multi skilled and adaptable.

During the course of a duty period, tasks have to be performed that one never ever imagined one finding oneself doing, nor ever been trained for. At Needles, we were fortunate to still have a solid fuel stove, a Rayburn, whilst elsewhere throughout the service, such facilities were being removed as part of modernisation. A decision had been made by Trinity House to remove our oven, such decision largely based upon the cost, bi annually, of servicing and rebricking ;it was also not uncommon to find that certain cast iron parts would often require replacing. In any offshore situation, costs of even the most simplest of tasks can be prohibitive and therefore serious prioritisation needs to be applied, with consideration be given as to the necessity of the task. We desperately fought to retain our Rayburn, arguing that, in addition to being an efficient means of cooking ,it's copper chimney, ascending the tower's height right up to the roof, provided an ambient heat which kept the whole lighthouse aired and free from damp and condensation; a compromise was reached. We would service, rebrick, order and fit spare parts to the solid fuel Rayburn, and in return, be allowed to keep it until such time as it became unsafe or beyond repair. With a little self training, plus a few phone calls to "people who knew about these things" we maintained our facility to the highest of standards, to the point of becoming "experts!"

To better retain the efficiency of our cooker ,it was essential that the chimney was regularly swept; this, in itself was a simple, yet quite unorthodox, operation, calling for good teamwork and timing. The copper chimney was approximately eight inches in diameter and rose some eighty feet in height; close to the top, an access trapdoor had been cut into the side, with a similar arrangement down at the base, adjacent to the Rayburn stove. The procedure for carrying out the cleaning operation went as follows; a long rope ,to which was attached a solid lead ball (cannon ball size!) was dropped from top to bottom down the chimney, clearing all in its' path! At the bottom, dust and coppered soot filled the air, with hopefully some soot finding it's way into the stoves' collecting tray. With the kitchen having firstly been cleared of all crockery e.t.c, the resulting required clean up, whilst still being a major undertaking, was at least, straightforward. This chimney cleaning operation was effected every two weeks during winter, that being the time when the Rayburn was in fullest use, with gas cooking in summertime. There was the odd occasion when the ball was dropped too soon sending soot and debris all over the kitchen ,but mostly the operation, with us having had so much practice went off well and the stove burnt more effectively than it had been doing.

As an afterthought, stations  which had their solid fuel stoves removed, soon observed increased levels of condensation, which despite various attempts at alleviating by the installation of alternative heating, was never quite fully resolved. Following automation, the situation worsened, requiring the use of dehumidifiers to reduce the dampness.

There were many and varied jobs similar to that above, such jobs were an essential part of life on an offshore Lighthouse but were not in the job description! An adaptable, flexible attitude to working practice formed an important part of a Lighthouse Keepers role, and ,in hindsight, I now realise just what was meant by the wording on the original application form which clearly stated the need for self reliance!

Annual Inspections by the Board of Trinity House, (the Elder Brethren), were, by their very nature, extremely and thoroughly carried out. Such inspections, were, after all, an endorsement, (or not!), of the efficiency and good order of an essential national navigational aid, and of the effectiveness of the crew responsible to maintain that aim. In previous pages I have mentioned in outline, the usefulness that we, as a crew found an inspection to be, and of our personal pride in being credited with an efficiently run station. During any such inspection, the visiting Board Members were rigorous in their checking and double checking all station systems, whilst satisfying themselves, quite rightly, that the Keepers on station were thoroughly acquainted and trained for the task required to keep the lighthouse in absolute A1 status. There was, however, one year, when we were almost "caught out" and our halos of efficiency came close to slippage. This involved the setting up of the "WR" navigation light fittings.

WR stands for War Regulation and requires certain modifications to be made, under Admiralty orders, to the way in which the main navigation lights are exhibited; it involves the setting up of shades and fittings which will obscure the light in particular directions making it visible only to shipping approaching from a prearranged and informed direction; i.e. convoys etc. Each lighthouse is equipped with a purpose designed set of WR fittings to be used in accordance with sealed orders which accompany the equipment. All WR fittings were kept in locked containers in a store as near as practicable to the main lantern area in readiness for use as and if required and all Keepers were to be trained in the use of such fittings. Somehow, with the passage of, thankfully, a lot of years of peace, and the need for such fittings therefore having diminished, such knowledge in the use of WR had slipped down the training list! This failing became only too apparent when on Needles in 1979 on an afternoon immediately preceding our inspection due early the following morning.

We had, for quite a number of days previously, checked and polished the entire lighthouse station in a manner even more thoroughly than that which was done every day, polish on polish, checks following more checks, and uniforms pristinely pressed to the point at which we stood proudly, and perhaps a little smugly, awaited the following day on which

64

to show off our station. Everything had been thought of, and no stone left unturned, or so we thought!

St Catherines' Lighthouse, just along the Isle of Wight shoreline from Needles, had had their inspection on the very day that we were congratulating ourselves on our gleaming and efficient station: one of the tasks they had been asked to perform was to demonstrate the rigging of the WR fittings; at this they admitted to having had some difficulty owing to their apparent lack of practice! To their credit they had passed the exercise to the Boards satisfaction, but it was only by a chance radio conversation that we had any inkling that WR was even on the agenda; even the "old hand" on station was taken by surprise. There was only one course of action that we could take, we could not risk failing! For more than three hours we rigged and dismantled the lens in readiness for inspection and for any war ever likely to break out between then and the following days' inspection; we became experts almost able to perform the task blindfolded! We were ready, and back to our previous state of satisfaction with an immense feeling of gratitude to our colleagues at St Catherines' for even mentioning the use of WR as part of the annual inspection.

The days approaching "Relief Day" were particularly busy with the crew implementing a further list of tasks to be effected; this period was known as the "relief clean", and the station, already bordering on immaculate and in service order, underwent an even more in depth going over. There were also certain tasks which only ever received attention at relief times; such works included washing the walls of every room and landing, stripping the lens mechanism for a thorough clean and regrease. Normal morning watch tasks continued as per standing orders, but with additional chores added .All engine oils were changed and diesel injectors renewed or cleaned, all fog signal equipment stripped and serviced, and, as already written about, the chimney swept!

Station paperwork, i.e. journal copies, stock returns e.t.c,. despite being attended to on a daily basis by the Keeper in Charge or Principal, now needed to be finalised; there being a surprising amount of essential papers which, following relief, were despatched to Trinity House. When a fairly junior ranked Keeper I was offered the chance to begin to learn to learn the required station paperwork, I, fortunately took up the offer ,little realising that, one day, I would be required to do it in a real situation; this came far sooner than originally expected when, due to sickness of the Principal Keeper, I found myself in charge and in at the deep end at Needles!

Amongst the more routine papers, for example, audit returns or fuel consumption and tank stock levels e.tc, there were written reports to submit regarding incidents in and around the station area, and also reports requesting the services of the various maintenance trades; there was also a requirement, at relief, for the on coming Keeper in Charge to sight, and sign for, the stations' stock of dangerous drugs (morphine e.tc).These drugs were stored in a secure cabinet adjacent to the main first aid supplies, and a copy of the most recently signed certificate of stock was sent ashore with the other station returns. A similar arrangement existed regarding the explosives stock (distress rockets e.t.c); this became even more acute with the escalation of hostility in Northern Ireland during the 1970,s. Any routine firing of a test/training flare or rocket had to meticulously reported both verbally at time of firing, and later in the form of a report stating dates, times and names of all present at exercise.

It was the responsibility of the Keeper in Charge of station to submit reports on any faults with station equipment, any arrivals or departures of personnel (ie Maintenance trades etc), during the duty turn; one perhaps somewhat unusual report was the quarterly submission of " Births, Deaths and Marriages." Should any member of the station complement had an addition or loss to his immediate family, or perhaps had recently married, then this information was required to be submitted to Trinity House.

During times of National Census, one could find oneself offshore on the relevant census date; it was the duty of the Keeper in Charge to ensure that all census forms were completed by those on board. Personally, my name forms part of the crew of Needles Lighthouse during such a census; the exact date of which, I do not now remember; I served at Needles from 1977-1983.

Stationed on a lighthouse, particularly a rock station, many of which had been built, over a century ago , it was not easy to never consider the extreme risk to shipping,that had existed prior to the establishment of a light, shipwreck and sailors terror being beyond our imagination. Each lighthouse was there to protect the mariner, but had probably only been built at the petitioned request of shipowners following serious shipwreck and loss of life; each location, therefore, had a litany of ships which had foundered amongst its' rocks. To the Lighthouse Keeper like myself, saddened as I was at the loss of so much life,the subject of shipwrecks was an intriguing history lesson and seemed to give our reasons for being there a deeper meaning. Viewing a wreck chart in any given area of coastline,is,in itself.a learning surprise; there are, in fact.so many wrecks it is almost hard to believe the reality; when one considers that these are only the KNOWN wrecks, it becomes even harder.In a time before modern communication, those ashore had little or no idea of the true position of shipping, and during fierce storms, even the ships' masters could easily lose sight of their real positions. Ships simply foundered, sailors perished, and all that could be concluded was, that the vessel was overdue and presumed lost,but where?

Diving as a leisure activity has increased in popularity in recent years; this in turn has increased the amount of "unknown wrecks being discovered, often by amateur leisure divers.Such discoveries have,by law, to be reported to the Receiver of Wrecks, as, despite the passage of time,most wrecks,do indeed,still belong to someone;this became apparent to us on Needles Lighthouse when a group of leisure divers researched and located the wreck of a 44 gun naval frigate, HMS Assurance, reportedly wrecked 24th April 1753.This wreck lay immediately off Needles point and literally right under the Lighthouse apparently in a deep rock gulley .Being a naval wreck, the vessel was still the property of the Crown,and in 1980 a Royal Naval Diving Party (HMS Dolphm,Portsmouth) commenced a site survey and investigation;to their credit,they invited the original leisure divers to assist in the venture.Investigations revealed a second wreck lying beside HMS Assurance,this find was another warship, the 38 gun frigate HMS Pomone which had hit the rocks on 11ᵗʰ October 1811. Of the two newly discovered wrecks,it was HMS Assurance which was to create the most interest for we,the watching Lighthouse crew.From deep in the depths came everything from musket shot to coinage,mostly "Pillar Dollars".This ship had been transporting the returning former Governor of Jamaica and his personal fortune of some £60,000 in coin,plus many collected artefacts. We ourselves witnessed the salvage of a most beautiful silver cherub tinder box and cigar case.The dive team would,on completion of a dive session,and in between tides,gather on the lighthouse landing and proceed to chip the concretion from their any finds;each find was carefully recorded,and the items secured aboard the attendant dive vessel.After that exercise was completed the divers would usually join us for a mug of lighthouse tea! The dive continued throughout three summers,during which our tours of duty months simply flew by, and our lighthouse was never short of company;! personally made several new friends of the diving team, whose skills I had ,on occasion, to call upon to free my jammed lobster pots!

One notable shipwreck in the Needles area was the Dutch East Indiaman "Campen," which foundered in 1627,and from which, divers recovered silver coinage and other artefacts. More recent history, 1947, saw the grounding and subsequent wrecking of the Greek steamer,"Varvassi" of 3,775 tons, just south of the lighthouse itself.In calm conditions and low tides, it is still possible to see the top of the vessels boilers, and part of the main engine, this wreckage has, on several occasions, been hit by small pleasure craft which have, unwittingly ventured too close ,and often at high speed. Whilst stationed at Needles, we have had to call the lifeboat to the aid of such casualties, who, fortunately without serious injury, have managed to scramble to the safety of the lighthouse or surrounding rocks; there was ,however, one potentially more serious incident,in which a large cruising yacht,on striking the boiler top debris,ripped her keel completely out of the hull.

I am, once again, pleased to be able to write of a safe result, as, although capsized, the craft remained afloat and all aboard were able to be rescued by Yarmouth lifeboat.

Such activity as the salvage diving, and, on a more sombre note, casualties to craft, made the Needles a particularly interesting posting with few "dull moments," and a wealth of marine archaeology, the progression of which we followed avidly. As the expeditions revealed ever more new findings, we were visited by Historians and others who had become involved at the request of the Diving Teams; several such archaeologists travelling from further up the Solent from the other side of the Isle of Wight, where they were involved in preparation work to raise the wreck of the "Mary Rose ." The lighthouse became a hive of activity, and Trinity House gave full permission for the teams to utilise the facilities, including the attachment of safety lines from the station boat landing, right down, and into the wreck site. This enabled the divers to literally "walk" down the guide rope unaffected by the often strong current around the rocks. A large yellow sign, prohibiting unlicenced and unauthorised divers, was attached to the lighthouse tower wall on the North facing side. After three seasons, full scale diving by the teams was scaled down, although, they admit, there remained much more to recover, and to learn, and hoped to return in the future.

Coins recovered from the wreck of the "Campen" were shown to us by the diving party as they progressed with their exploration; we on the lighthouse, followed their progress with great interest throughout subsequent diving seasons.

In March 1983, I was transferred from Needles to that of the "pool" of Lighthouse Keepers, this was a group of Assistant Keepers not assigned to any particular lighthouse, but, who would travel on relieving duties wherever cover was required. This situation came about because automation had seen the withdrawal of Keepers on various stations, thus creating a surplus of manpower. It was decided by the Board that every Keeper would undertake a year in the "pool" at some point; sad as I was at leaving the Needles, I consoled myself in the fact that I would get my "pool" service over with sooner, rather than later. I had, after all,enjoyed my own station at Needles for over five years, so felt no real reason in complaining!

My pool service took me to Flatholm, Inner Dowsing, Wolf Rock and others including Round Island (Isles of Scilly), where I was fortunate in serving six months; this in effect, was akin to having my own station again!

In February 1984, more instructions, my pool time being over, I was to be transferred to Casquets Lighthouse, Channel Islands. Good news, indeed!!


I took up my appointment at Casquets Light House, joining station in March 1984, I remained until the Light House became automated in Nov 1990; Casquets, having been manned since 1724, it became my personal claim to fame in being the very last Lighthouse Keeper "up the ladder" upon the station becoming computer controlled.

Les Casquets, to give it it's full Norman-French title, lies approximately seven and a half miles to the South East of the Island of Alderney, and seventeen miles North of Guernsey.

In the original construction of Casquets, there had been three lighthouse towers, each illuminated by a coal fired beacon housed in fire baskets known as a cresset. Each of the three towers had a name, St Peters, St Thomas, and Le Dungeon; St Peters tower become home to the main navigation light, the remaining two were part demolished to a third of their original height. On top of the old St Thomas tower, a helipad was constructed, whilst Le Dungeon housed the station Engine Room; all functions of which, in addition to the main light , were monitored via a control panel within our main quarters. Quite a novelty after my service on Tower Rocks!

*LES CASQUETS LIGHTHOUSE .*
*NOTE REMAINS OF THREE TOWERS*

The French coast being some eighteen miles to the South, and mostly, plainly visible,gave Casquets an almost "colonial" feel. Reliefs were carried out by helicopter, thus ensuring that one arrived on-shore feeling "civilised", and with one's uniform still looking clean and pressed; this, quite a contrast to the regular soakings experienced on winter time Needles boat reliefs ! Travel to and from station was very straightforeword; by taking a flight from Exeter or Plymouth, both airports being within easy reach of my home,I always arrived in Guernsey the day prior to relief. This afforded me ample time to arrange food supplies etc. Channel Island lighthouses were efficiently served by a local agent based at Guernsey airport, to whom we reported for any pre relief information and briefings.My transfer to Casquets gave me the chance to fully experience "how the other half lived " and I could not help but compare it with life on the Towers.

The Lt Hse station was constructed some 25 metres above sea level, on a rocky islet 350 metres in length, and 175 metres wide,.A Class 2 Rock Station, accommodation, in estate agent terminology was,a 4 bedroom cottage, boas ting kitchen, bathroom, lounge and dining room, with a level walk to all amenities,i.e. Engine Room etc. We enjoyed single bed room status, each equipped with "real " furniture including the luxury of a divan bed. Next to our, the Keepers, abode, was another cottage used by any visiting maintenance personnel, this dwelling also, being self contained with all facilities. There were various out-buildings, workshop, engine room e.t.c. all contained within a walled compound, giving an almost fortress feeling.To quote the words of one wit, "twinned with Alcatraz !" Until the early 1800's, Keepers and their families had lived on the island, both raising and educating their children there; and, when necessary, travelling to Alderney in their own sail-boat to collect supplies,further supplementing their needs by fishing, and growing what vegetables they could.The remains of the old gardens was enough to realise just how hard they would have needed to work in order to produce any crops of real value. Harvested seaweed was used in order to provide much needed fertilizer.

During World War two, the Station was occupied by German Forces who operated a forward Signal Station from Casquets, and we often found debris left from those years, this included old ammunition and shell cases etc. There are some interesting accounts of British commando raids on Casquets, and we were privileged, on one occasion, to welcome one former commando, a Mr Tom Winter, who, as a guest of Trinity House, had returned to look at the Island, his previous visit having been as a young man scaling the rocks from a cold, wet rubber dinghy, under cover of darkness, and with the ever present risk of discovery by the enemy.

*LES CASQUETS MONORAIL TRAIN (WAS ALWAYS ON TIME!)*

Life on Casquets was a real "step up" in standards of life aboard a lighthouse. We were high up, on a rocky island with accommodation and other buildings constructed around a central courtyard area. At "class 2" rock status it was high in amenity value!   .

We, the keepers, lived in what had once been the Principal Keepers cottage; this affording us much more space than was common in most lighthouses. For myself, having, prior to Casquets, had to sleep in a "banana bunk" on offshore stations, I now found myself with my own bedroom and comfortable REAL bed! Just along the hall was the bathroom!

Domestically, we enjoyed a spacious TV lounge,  adjoined by a large kitchen and dining room, it was all a far off world from the lack of privation shared by the tower rock lighthouses. I felt more than justified in having no guilty feelings, now being aboard such a well appointed station; having previously completed six years at Needles Lighthouse, and grown to know each and every one of its' stairs personally!

Our watchkeeping hours, work routines, and cooking arrangements were, on Casquets, very similar to that of all other Trinity House Lighthouses, but, in addition, we were a designated Trinity House Signal station responsible for the coordination of signal traffic for other stations within the "Casquets Group." The group was made up of Les Hanois Lighthouse (west of Guernsey), Royal Sovereign Lighthouse (12 miles south of Sussex coast), and Channel Lightvessel (mid English Channel). From these stations, all messages and signals were transmitted to Casquets for collation and onward transmission to Trinity House, at E. Cowes. This aspect of lighthouse routine duties formed an interesting "extra," which, whilst often making our station a busy one, meant that we were in touch with our colleagues on other stations, several times per day. Any items of service news was rapidly dispatched around the group, such information offering new inspiration for dinner table debate!

The Channel Lightvessel was, as with ourselves, relieved by Trinity House helicopter via Guernsey airport, and it was our responsibility at Casquets to radio monitor the helicopter operation throughout until relief was completed. This was an essential health and safety issue, as helicopter operations on lightvessels meant having to land upon a ship as it pitched and rolled unpredictably.

In all but the very worst of weather conditions, it was possible to take a walk for exercise, and, with the engine room being remote from the other main buildings, little or no engine noise was imposed upon we, the crew; the fog horn, however, did have one of its' trumpets pointing down across the island and right over our heads!

An "Island Rock " Station, by it's very nature and area size, afforded much more space in which to provide, not just a higher standard of "creature comfort" but far greater protection from the elements. On Casquets, we were much less vulnerable to the winter weather than our Tower Rock counterparts; our Island offering a natural breakwater against the worst affects of high seas. This belief was shattered on a night in October 1989, the night of the hurricane!

in In preparation for my duty on the "middle watch" (0000-0400) at midnight, I had "turned" to bed at shortly after 2200, but, was awakened only one hour later, by the loud howling of wind, and crashing seas, far in excess of any normal storm. What sounded like gravel stones were hitting the bedroom window, and the wind, whistling through the helipad netting, played a loud, high pitched wailing tune,· which, despite my having served some three years on station, I had never ever, heard before. Feeling, to say the least, a little uneasy, at eleven fifteen, I got up, and made my way to the watchroom. I was joined soon afterwards by my other colleague, who had also got up to investigate. The Keeper on watch was pleased to see us, as he watched the weather deteriorate, and the barometer crash, for the previous hour or so. This was no "normal" gale by any standard, and I could feel, within myself, a fear of the sea, that I had never before experienced; my two colleagues were unusually quiet, except for certain expletives voiced when another mountainous wave thundered against the building.

As the minutes passed, so the storm seemed to worsen; glancing out of the windows, we could see the raging sea rushing and swirling in the yard outside; it roared, its, reflection almost glowing in a phosphorescent white cauldron, as the lighthouse beams played upon it. It was if the sea was running literally up the island and across the top; we could hear loose stonework being thrown around outside our main door. For some 35 minutes, this continued, whilst we inside, could only wait in the hope that all would turn out safely; the anemometer showing the wind speed as 108 mph and then nothing! The wind cups having parted company with the tower roof! Every now and again, we could see the twinkling of ships lights through the spray; I remember thinking, please God help them in what they must be going through. We began to try to watch the late film on television, only to miss the ending when our t.v. arial broke away and headed rapidly up channel!

Shortly after what had seemed like hours in time, but, in fact for what had been only some 40 minutes, the noise and the clatter gave way to almost silence, all becoming eerily still, as the low pressure which brought its' storm, moved on up the channel, taking its' sting, and our fear with it!

The precursor to our night of nature at its, very worse, had, with hindsight, been touched upon earlier the previous evening. We had sat and listened to Mr Michael Fish, the weatherman, on television, he jovially having informed us that, whilst "gales were forecast, viewers needn,t worry about anything like a hurricane!" Apparently, a viewer had written in, concerned that one was expected. I,m sure that he will never forget that particular weather forecast! I, for one, most certainly won't!

Following an unnerving time after the storms' passing, we ventured out in the uncanny quiet of the early morning, to inspect for damage, which, apart from having lost some stonework and concrete areas of the landing, was, thankfully, minimal. The yard was full of seaweed, stones and broken driftwood, and our R/T arial requiring a hasty repair before we were able to report our situation to our "folks at home" and also to Trinity House. We contacted the Channel Lightvessel stationed some 20 miles to our North; it being they who had experienced the storm firsthand in every sense of the word, they had, thankfully, safely come through it. The crew told of how the ship had, at times, gone over on her beam, at an angle never previously experienced, but had simply bounced back up for more !Apart from much broken crockery, and a few bruises with the crew being tossed about, they were happy and safe! A credit to all who designed and built her, (Philip and Sons, Dartmouth, Devon), and to the crew who manned her in such atrocious conditions.

A week later following the storm, I flew into Guernsey on my relief and could clearly see the devastation across the island; huge greenhouses twisted and bent, and houses with canvas over roofs, clearly makeshift repairs following what had, apparently been, the highest winds for almost a century.

From early on in 1990, work commenced on the automation of Casquets, from which time on, our complement was increased from there being just we three Keepers, to there then being a cross section of trade technicians, often numbering as many as 12 or more. Much structural alteration was undertaken, to allow the squads of Trinity Hse Engineers, Electricians and " Boffins " to continue their installation work. For our part, we enjoyed their companionship, and, everyone, without exception, worked congenially alongside one another, often enjoying, many a "good laugh". It was essential that normal Lt House watch-keeping routine was maintained until the very last day of manned operation, whereupon it's control and monitoring would be undertaken by Computer link from nearby Alderney .

Outside of working hours, we enjoyed inter-departmental fishing, skittles and badminton competitions, the latter two being held in the yard. That summer was particularly hot, and most meals were taken communally outside on the heli-deck. From redundant timber packaging we constructed a large picnic table, and, it was not uncommon for us to be outside enjoying the sunshine well into the evening. A further enterprise, was the weekly barbecue, usually held on a Saturday evening, everyone contributing to the menu and it's preparation. When bad weather prevented outside entertainment, games of cards. Trivial Pursuit e.t.c. were organised indoors, again, often on an inter-departmental basis, with an individual champion being declared fortnightly.

Casquets was reknowned for being the only lighthouse within our service that possessed its' own train; this being a mono rail constructed to transport goods etc in the event of having to use the lower (sea level) helipad. This helicopter pad facility only ever being brought into use in the event of particularly heavy loads, and proving invaluable during later automation works.

Once having settled in to life on Casquets, and having spent my first duty turn familiarising myself with station equipment etc, it was time, with Spring upon us, to seriously begin checking the fishing prospects. Casquets being part of such a large rocky reef, it seemed a fair assumption that the area would be home to crabs, lobsters etc, and therefore time for me to set about constructing the necessary crab pots and getting them into the water as soon was possible.

Casquets, being a large station, had a wealth of storage space, this being so meant that, unlike on towers, any materials left over by maintenance teams upon completion of works, were stored for use in the future.In addition to this, because of the high costs of helicopter transport, much material which would otherwise have been taken ashore, was now simply surplus, and of no real future usage value .It was from this source that I was able to construct my crab pots; using steel reinforcing mesh, (left over from helideck works), to form the main framework, I covered the outside by utilising old netting found amongst the rocks at low tide. In order to begin fishing as quickly as possible, my early pots were hastily constructed, but at least were moderately successful in catching crabs and the odd lobster; it was , however, during the following winter that I really began to apply skills taught me by my fishing family forbears. By stripping down redundant station polypropylene rope and braiding new net from the resultant twine, by springtime I had acquired some seventy five feet of netting, more than adequate to cover my Mark 2 design, streamlined fish traps, this time bigger and of more durable construction than my earlier efforts. By Easter of that year, (1985), I had six, ready to fish, new pots; by fishing no more than two at a time, I always had good opportunity to keep them in good repair.The rugged reefs of Casquets, took their toll of chafing damage upon my home made pots; the results, however, more than compensating for the work, (and fun!) involved in the operation.

Crabs would be boiled and the white meat frozen in redundant margarine tubs retained for the purpose; after all who wished to eat had done so, there was always ample stock to be able to take home in a cool bag. My record take home was 27 lb of white crab meat, and 20 lobsters (boiled and frozen whole), this following a one month turn of duty; Casquets had proved to be a good provider !

In spring and summer, bass and Pollack provided good sport and healthy eating, whilst the deep gullies around the rocks were perfect for my pots, and also excellent places in which to lay multi hook longlines. These lines yielded conger eel and often wrasse, the latter providing further crab pot bait! Conger would be cured in our home made smoke oven thus transforming an otherwise unpopular eating fish into a first rate culinary delicacy!

Fishing on most Lighthouses often meant having to compete with the local seal population, who, I have to admit, were much better at it than I ! Apart from their besting us at fishing, they did provide us with much amusement as they effortlessly sped through the often choppy sea around us. After all, they were there long before we were!

Wasn't it a bit boring? is often asked of me ! The short answer given in one word is a resounding NO !How can it be when, out on the Lighthouse, time for oneself is so readily available.

Out on Casquets ,using materials left from a stone Masons' maintenance trip, we constructed a smoke oven in the old garden area. The oven was of brick construction with a steel door at one end. Complete with metal pipe work chimney ,the whole structure resembled a small boiler. The expertise in its operation and management came courtesy of our then Principal Keeper, Norman W ,who hailed from the channel island of Sark ,on which smoke ovens were apparently much used .He explained that, at home they fuelled the oven with gorse, but ,in our situation ,we would experiment with whatever was available wood wise; this we found in abundance in the form of driftwood! Provided that we ensured that our timber was free from paint etc ,we chopped it up and utilised it! Our smoke oven was a remarkable success and improved the flavour of much of our fishing catches ;our menu now affording smoked mackerel, conger (highly delicious!) and Pollack. Once the fish had been cleaned, filleted ,and set within the smoker ,it was often left to process for up to 24 hours ,during which time, it became a task of the keeper coming off watch to tend the fire before adjourning to bed At low tides, we would forage for driftwood in readiness for the next "firing up" of our creation, whilst at mealtimes, our diets become gourmet experiences.

To continue on the summer theme, it was a pleasure to be able to partake of good sea air with fine calm picture postcard seas ;that after what could often be long ,dark, storm lashed days of winter. The sea so often looked so inviting for a swim, although of course, out of the question amongst the strong tides and currants surrounding our environment ,except, that is, when stationed at Casquets.

At the southern of the island was a deep, narrow gulley ,surrounded on three sides by the granite rock which made up our island; it extended some 20 metres in length by approx 10 metres width and was very deep at high tide. At low water, with the granite exposed to the warm sunshine, the rocks heated, which, in turn warmed the incoming sea ;result, a  very pleasant and refreshing swim .With the western, open end of the "west gut "as it was known, being roped across for safety ,our summers were to be greatly enjoyed. When having on board, visiting maintenance teams ,a swimming gala was often organised, often followed by a barbeque of smoked fish shellfish and salad .To ensure fairness to all on station on such occasions, the watch keeping duties would be shared to enable all to enjoy the feast. This kind of event originated with the arrival of the additional personnel ,on station to carry out automation conversion works .In the final summer of works, our complement often numbered twelve or more; this ensured a delightful atmosphere, not only at a barbeque event, but throughout the project.

That summer turned out  be one of the hottest and prolonged and, without really trying, we all boasted good tans .I recall how ,one of the project teams, having served some six weeks on station, went ashore on leave,only to be met by their boss, who, on noticing their bronzed appearance commented that they couldn't have done as much work as they perhaps ought. Their reply was simply that, having had one hours' lunch break outside each day, forty two hours of hot sun was more than enough to tan anyone! Not being able to refute their reasoning, he just muttered something and walked away!

Our "Barbie" was a complete success, and, we at Casquets could justifiably claim to be the first, and perhaps only, lighthouse in the

United Kingdom, to add barbeque brickettes to our supply order for the next visiting helicopter!

With so many on station, the ingenuity of ideas was amazing; one reads tales of how, in POW camps, the incarcerated servicemen would find and use skills they had never previously known about, and from which they would produce goods and documents that passed the closest of scrutiny. In our own simpler way, our own pool of ideas did likewise . Our barbeque itself was constructed from an old portable steel workbench and a redundant electrical switch box! The holes that once served to access cables, now allowed the necessary level of draught in order that our steaks were done to the satisfaction of their waiting customers!

On an off-shore Lighthouse, deliveries of fuel and lubrication oils, coal and water e.t.c. were serviced by a specialist fleet of Trinity House vessels or tenders, which, regionally based, tended the requirements of all Lighthouses, Light-vessels and Buoys within a given area. Upon my entry into the Service, the Trinity House tender fleet numbered six, but, with the increased use of helicopters, and the on-going programme of Light House automation, the fleet became reduced to number two large vessels, supported by a "mini-fleet" of port based smaller craft.

The arrival at Station of the supply tender, heralded a day or more of intense activity on any Light House. Landing cranes / hoists and mooring ropes were rigged to assist the tender's launches as they ferried in the Station's supplies, operating a shuttle service between the larger Tender, anchored as near as safely practical, and the Light House landing. On larger stations, such as Island rocks, as much as 20,000 gallons of fuel would be delivered, 250 gallons per trip per launch, with several thousand gallons of fresh water being landed at the same rate simultaneously. Because of it's vulnerability to weather and sea conditions, on completion of operations, all landing equipment, crane hoists, mooring lines e.t.c. had to be dismantled, cleaned and serviced, and stowed away inside the Lighthouse, each item of gear being made ready for immediate future usage. A regular part of Light House routine, in the days of full manning, was a "rigging drill/' usually once a month, which ensured that all station personnel were fully familiar with the intricate rigging assembly of all boat landing equipment and it's maintenance.

Landings were regularly cleaned with chloride of lime to control weed growth, thus ensuring a safe, non-slip surface, and all external landing fittings, bollards, mooring rings e.t.c. were kept thoroughly cleaned and greased. It had always to be borne in mind, that, as well as such landing equipment being essential for delivery purposes, it might equally be needed for use of the evacuation of a sick or injured colleague, or, maybe even one self! .In the ideal scheme of things, a helicopter would more than likely be summoned to effect any necessary rescue, but one always needed to allow for the potential interference of "Murphy's Law!" In an isolated situation such as an off-shore Light House, where landings are, to say the least dangerous, one needed to be  feel safely dependent on colleagues to ensure a safe and co-ordinated work effort.

All Keepers were required to be competent in the making up and splicing of mooring ropes and loading strops which were often used under high strain, and under conditions of heavy weather and sea conditions. When winching heavy, often bulky, equipment, good ropework skills were essential, both for the safety of those on the landing, and those in the even more dangerous location in the launch , often several metres beneath the crane. My own previous career had already taught me necessary knot and splicing skills, but, with potential Lt Hse Keepers hailing from all walks of life, good training in rigging skills was paramount. It was for this purpose that Trinity House operated a Training School at Blackwall, London, at which all new entrants to the Service were instructed and examined in these relevent skills, prior to further practical training at a Lighthouse.

Commodities such as drinking water, so often taken for granted when at home, took on a different priority when on an offshore lighthouse; the storage capacities of many stations were not large and therefore called for the good use of "consumer common sense"

Tower rock lighthouses had relatively small storage capacity and relied upon good weather in enabling a boat delivery. On Needles, for example, our water tank could only hold some 1400 gallons of water when brim full; to the layman this might seem a good amount, but, when shared between three, or sometimes more personnel, is not an excessive amount per person taking into account the need for domestic cleaning, meal dishes and laundry etc! Fortunately on Needles, the toilet was flushed by sea water from a storage tank pumped full every few days or so, weather permitting!

During winter months, deliveries of fresh water could often prove difficult due to poor weather conditions; during such times, the uncertainty of water delivery dictated the need for very careful conservation until the tank could be filled again .There was one occasion during my time at Needles that due to extremely prolonged poor sea conditions, our water supply storage came very close to running out completely ;it was only thanks to our own local boatman, who, running in with a fast inflatable, was able to hastily deliver a few 5 gallon containers full. These had to be thrown up to waiting hands as the craft flew past on the surf. This lifeline of drinking water kept the kettle and teapot topped until some days later, in better conditions, the Trinity House tender was able to attend and refill our tank to capacity. Such problems were only the lot of offshore towers; on larger stations all was quite different!

Having served at Needles for almost six years, my acquired water conserving education had been an often hard lesson; my transfer to Casquets however ended such thinking! Casquets had an almost limitless capacity of fresh water as , being on an island which had many years past, housed families, we could store some 20,000 gallons of drinking water, added to which we could collect and store a further 25,0000 gallons of rain water .

From the roofs of each of three cottage sized dwellings, the rain water was channelled ,via the paved yard area, into two large collecting tanks.

It was part of the duty keepers routine, during appropriate rainfall, to open the downpipe valves so as to collect any rainfall; before doing so, we always allowed the first hour or so of rain to run away to waste. After checking the clarity of the water by means of a glass, and, sometimes sipping it to check for salt content, then, and only then, did we deem the water worthy of collection. This water, classified as for domestic use, as opposed to fresh, served as bathwater ,toilet flushing and for all station cleansing duties including supplying the station washing machine! A far cry from virtual rationing as had to be the case on towers!

From having to use sea borne craft to deliver essential supplies such as water, the construction of helipads enabled delivery by air; this involved the use of "pillow tanks", each containing some 250 gals of water (or diesel fuel), being landed onto the roof level helipad, from where it was gravity fed to the tanks below. As part of almost every monthly relief, each station would receive a regular delivery by air,and the keepers no longer had to worry over perhaps enjoying that extra shower or two!

Before continuing further, I would like to impart a few reflections upon Christmas time on a Lighthouse, as, I have always felt that this was the duty turn when most,myself included,seriously questioned, if only for a moment, the wisdom of choosing our particular career.

Countless numbers of people are obliged to work at Christmas,but most,at least are able to rejoin their families at some time during the festive day; not so the offshore Lighthouse Keeper. It was often the case that,having left home in mid December,all thoughts of Christmas had been long forgotten by the time that we returned home in mid January,indeed,most of the best sale bargains too, had long since been snapped up!

On station,the festive season,in my experience,never passed without due celebration, and, once having ensured that all station duties were maintained as normal, we always managed a hearty traditional meal with all the trimmings.Such a meal,as in any household,required effective forward planning,except that our meal had to be ordered,packed and then delivered,all in one piece by either boat or helicopter.To acheive this,each of the three members of the Lt Hse crew would,by mutual agreement,undertake responsibility for one particular item of the menu,i.e.one would order and ensure delivery of the turkey,another the pudding,e.t.c so that,come the pre-festive relief day,no one individual had it all to do.The total cost of the Christmas provisions were then shared equally between the three crew,this being probably the only single occasion during the Lt Hse year, when messing arrangements would be pooled in such a way.

Come Christmas day,there was never any reluctance on anyones part in volunteering to be "cook of the day" the only main stipulation being that the 0400-1200,duty Keeper would put the turkey in early during his watch period,and see that it was regularly checked and basted! The real gastronome would then attend to the rest later.We enjoyed some splendid Festive lunches cooked to perfection by dedicated would-be chefs,with the washing up willingly dealt with by those "who also served" in a real team spirit. I remember particularly one Christmas on Casquets, when the full menu and lunch itinary was published on the mess room door,and how surprised I was that we had gained a fish course, some petit fours and a splendid cheese board selection, all these extras having been laid on as a goodwill surprise by the volunteer chef of the day, Principal Keeper Brian Harris, of whom it must be said was an excellent cook who always seemed to thoroughly enjoy creating interesting meals, whether for all of us, or for just himself. I still possess and cherish that published menu amongst my Light House memorabilia and, although I have always enjoyed pleasant Light House Christmases wherever I have served, that particular Casquets Christmas Day will always,for me, remain the most memorable of all.I feel that I should also give mention to my other colleague on that occasion, Assistant Keeper, Tony Wibberley, sadly now passed on, who liberally provided the after dinner brandy and cigars as his gift to us in the true spirit of comradeship. And my surprise for the boys? the answer is a home cooked and fully decorated Christmas cake, prepared by my wife and presented to the crew, with due ceremony at tea time, at the conclusion of a day positively alive with "goodwill towards men," well, three of us anyway!

Christmas on an offshore Light House was not simply one of three Lighthouse Keepers making the best of not being at home with their families, nor just of the spirit of comradeship in shared isolation, it was of sharing, at least in mind Christmas with countless individuals, country wide who had sent us cards and best wishes, often simply addressed to, for example, The Keepers, Such & such Light House, We received greetings from maritime organisations, ship ping companies, schools, and private individuals, many living far, far from the sea, but who, for their own private reasons, wished us to know that they would be thinking of us during our Christmas vigil. We received parcels of festive fayre from yachting clubs, ships masters and fishermen, most of whom were unknown to us by name, but to whose vessels we had perhaps waved ,or heard on the radio as they proceeded on passage .We always endeavoured, at the first opportunity, to send thank you letters and belated greetings, this responsibility also being equally shared between each of our three crew members on station.

My most poignant Christmas tide memory is of late one Christmas Eve at Casquets ,whilst sitting alone in the watchroom, feeling just a little sorry for myself,and more than just a little homesick. With the time approaching midnight, and soon time to wake the next Keeper for his duty,the V.H.F. radio, channel 16 was quiet, save only for the inevitable crackle. Picking up the microphone, I wished anyone listening a "Merry Christmas" from the Casquets Lt Hse.What followed were greetings in so many different languages from so many different ships, continuing for well over five minutes; I felt positively moved, and no longer so alone. Even though I could not identify most of the languages,I knew that each in their own way, they were wishing me what I had wished to them. What had previously been just ships lights in the night, were now people just like me,a long way from home on Christmas night.I found the experience overwhelming, and recall it to mind often,it being my long held belief that,irrespective of flag or religion, there exists a bond between all men of the sea, a belief which my experience of that Christmas Eve fortifies.

Christmases on a Lt Hse were of three men simply getting on with the job in hand just as on any other day, but with the one exception in that this day harboured individual, very private thoughts, and very public outward sentiments of comradeship. Interestingly, some of our first telephoned Christmas Day greetings, came from Keepers whose good fortune it was to be home on leave with their families, yet. whose empathy was with us on that day.

New Years Eve was usually toasted in by all, and warm handshakes exchanged with the inevitable observation that "this year we'll be home for Christmas!" With the introduction of a new calender, relief dates for the coming year were hastily marked off, and copies taken for use by those at home.As the festive season faded away, then so were dismantled the station Christmas tree and decorations. By relief day all had reverted back to normal status and all thoughts directed towards being home again, another turn completed!Being posted offshore remains for me, a most valued experience, during which, despite being far removed from "civilisation," we had opportunities presented us which I feel, in their own way ,compensated for our remote situation .I refer, in particular, to the quality "me time," which, in so called, normal life ,is often difficult to find. I would be the first to admit that, when home on leave ,the last thing one should be doing is ignoring the family and burying ones' face in a book or other hobby. Out on" the rock," it was essential to follow some kind of interest whether that was simply watching TV ,reading or perhaps listening to music.(The walkman with headphones was a much valued toy when on out station). There were however, countless other opportunities and hobbies exercised by myself and fellow Keepers; I have already mentioned ships in bottles and lamp bulbs, in addition to which I would add ,knot display boards, at which I became quite adept. If one so wished, there would always be someone ashore who would offer to buy a lighthouse made knot board to hang on their wall. Personally, I only ever sold one ,the rest I gave to family and friends, my fun lay in making and displaying knotting skills! Hobbies abounded!

When on Casquets and following completion of work by some maintenance carpenters, I was fortunate in obtaining some quality plywood, the end result from which, being my first lighthouse made dolls house. Making it turned out to be the easiest part, as travelling from Channel Isles to home on a commercial aircraft had its problems when wishing to transport a three bedroom house as part of my personal luggage. Airport security, with whom we ,as Lighthouse crew enjoyed a good working relationship, thought it hilarious ,and a "first" for them when I tried to explain what was in the box! Subsequent dolls houses ,and there were several,(family/friends orders),travelled flat packed to be finally assembled on arrival at home!

Lighthouses proved to be first class locations in which to study ,and many Keepers, myself included, took up courses, the Open University, and other such correspondence courses proving popular. For myself, I studied Social Science with the O.U. and attended the appropriate summer schools during my leave period. Although posting items of coursework was difficult, all such correspondence schools made great allowances for our location.

One former colleague ,very worthy of note, was a Principal Keeper on Needles, who spent a lot of hours in recording talking books for the blind. The RNIB provided him with all necessary equipment enabling him to record some first class literature for visually impaired listeners. Sadly, the gent in question is no longer with us ,but I understand that he received several commendations for his work. There were others, of course, for whom hobbies meant being involved in more sporty entertainment; by this I refer to Golf ,yes, Golf!!

At Casquets, our Principal Keeper, Brian ,constructed, with our help, a driving range ,in which to practice his golf swing. This was manufactured by slinging netting over a framework made from scaffolding stored on station; this was rigged up in the lower station yard During times of bad weather , Brian would move indoors and putt along the bedroom passageway, a carpet tiled floor area some thirty feet or so in length! Brian contended that it was his hours of lighthouse golf practice that was greatly responsible in lowering his personal handicap ,he subsequently became Captain of Freshwater ,IOW ,Golf Club! It was Brian, who, incidently had, some years previously, been my PK at Needles during that memorable summer of '76

There were, apparently other golfers,on Tower Rocks, who managed a few practice shots by tying elastic to the ball and teeing off on the helideck!

During the summer months of 1990, automation works continued apace, with helicopters arriving with frequent deliveries of new equipment and plant necessary to keep the schedule within deadlines. We, the Keepers, watched as our station gradually became controlled by silicon chips.

It has often been mentioned by those involved in previous automation schemes, that with so many personnel on station,, and with the unavoidable noise and inconvenience that such a major scheme necessitates, that a certain acrimony has developed between the Lt Hse Keepers ,till having to continue their job, and the Installation team trying to simultaneously progress with theirs. On Casquets, even on the most difficult days of noise and heavy labour, we all coexisted as one big "happy family ," within which, a happy and healthy atmosphere nurtured itself, and some firm friendships becoming established. Even today, Casquets is still looked back on with affection, by literally all of us who served or worked there; a " one off" is one expression I have heard used to describe it.

By the Autumn of 1990, it became very apparent that it would not be long before the computer gained full control; various Station functions were already operating on a semi-automatic test basis though under the 24 hr supervision of the Duty-Keepers! The long established, air driven Fog-horn which had earned a reputation as being one of the loudest and least Keeper ~ friendly in the Service, had now been superseded by an electronic replacement, which caused no interuption whatsoever to peaceful sleep Now that the house was about to be vacated, the noisy neighbour had become politely quiet ! As the final days of manning approached, we all began to speculate as to our next respective Stations, each of us having our private favourite choices It came to our crew to be the last ever to man the Casquets, a date for final computer takeover having been fixed. We simply could not let such a milestone in Lt Hse history just pass into oblivion, without some sort of sense of due occasion, and set about the organisation of our pre-automation eve party. The wife of one of the Commissioning Engineers kindly despatched a " Casquets cake " via her old man; (thank you Mrs Potter!), and anyone who could legitimately " wangle " a return trip to the Stn for the purpose of " final adjustment, " did their best to be there for the occasion. Amidst great ceremony, and with associated speeches and toasts, the Ensign was symbolically lowered, as the sun set over "our Empire !" We had contacted B.B.C.TV South West ,who gave the imminent demanning ,a mention on it's regional news bulletin. With the party over, the following morning we, the Keepers, left station for the last time, ending an era.For myself, I left the Casquets with much apprehension, but also with some fond memories of a well run, happy, station, shared with  some very sincere people. So, it was home for a month's leave ,with Xmas included, then a transfer to Start Point, back to where I'd started !

# SECTION THREE
# LIGHTHOUSE LIFE CHANGES; KEEPER TO COMPUTER

My transfer to Start Point meant a complete change of lifestyle for me, as, after a career spent "on the rocks", Start, was a land station and was thus operated in a completely different way. I have to admit to feeling more than a little apprehensive regarding the prospect !

The year was 1990, and with the automation of Casquets completed, the Service was then reduced to a mere five off-shore Lighthouses, and therefore another off-shore appointment was out of the question; we were literally running out of places to go ! There had also, by then, been two rounds of redundancies,. which, fortunately had been taken up by early retirements and those wishing to take voluntary severance; the year 2000 was being projected as the then deadline for the completion of the automation programme, and it was being predicted that the first of the compulsory redundancies would not be too far into the future. In this climate of such grave uncertainty, I accepted my new station readily ! There is, however, an interesting story as to how a vacancy occurred at Start Pt, a story that is, quite literally a moving one !

Unlike the rocks, Keepers at Land stations lived, on station, with their families, each station having a group of cottages attached for their use, staff, as with their off-shore counterparts, consisting of a Principal Keeper, in charge, and two or three Assistant keepers. Children attended school locally, although the term locally often required a two mile walk to the nearest bus stop, followed by a far longer ride to school than their classmates from town. The Keepers at Land stations had an annual leave entitlement of 4/5 weeks in a similar way to "civvy" workers; Keepers wives being free to take up local employment if they so desired. This then, is the framework into which I was to be placed, a way of life so completely different to that off-shore, and, with noticeably far less perks, i.e. leave, for one's trouble !! Oh yes, and just how did the vacancy arise ? well, quite simply, one of the Keepers cottages slipped over the cliff, (fortunately whilst they were out ! ) leaving the station needing a Keeper but having no where, on station for him to live. Who was not only available, but lived just a half hour drive away ? Yours truly ! Thus I was appointed A.K. Start Point on a "live out" basis, two days on duty, and two days off ! I was pleased to accept, and became Senior Assistant Keeper.

Once into the routine, I felt quite contented with my new situation and seemed to be always at home this lead me to ponder that perhaps there is something to be said for regular hours for the family man after all. For my wife, it meant that chores such as mowing the lawn e.t.c. became more of an equally shared responsibility, rather than a singular toil enforced by employment circumstances. Despite living off-station, except on duty periods, I was still never made to feel anything other than a full member of the team by my colleagues. This was something of particular importance to me, as this question of integration had been a source of my doubt as to whether or not I should in fact take up Start Point as an appointment. I also knew that an automation date just two years hence had been set, but, was more than happy in the meantime at being so close to home. This, to me, was a bonus to be enjoyed whilst the opportunity prevailed!

Despite my earlier scepticism, Start Point turned out for me, to be a happy appointment; it is South Devons' most southerly point, and set in particularly beautiful, unspoilt, surroundings; in spring,the headland is a carpet of bluebells and primroses, the scent from which could be experienced right down to almost sea level. Such an environment was a mecca for walkers and others, both local and visitor alike, and for myself, pure joy in nature at its' finest. Having spent so much time off-shore, I had given little thought to the enjoyment of shore-based nature! It was not uncommon to see foxes and badgers around the Lt House compound,, and we paid particular attention to a pair of peregrine falcons who had chosen to nest on a cliff ledge within our boundary. Needless to add, birdwatchers were enthralled!

Being a land station, permission was granted by Trinity House to open the Lt House to the visiting public during daylight, non-operational hours. Visitors were pleased to be able to climb the stairways and actually be able to view a working Lt House from the inside, whilst we, its' crew, did our best to explain to them how both the Lt House and the Service operated. Trinity House generously supplied information factsheets and we ourselves made up some explanatory display boards showing dates and locations of some of Start Points' shipwrecks. We received groups from schools, colleges e.t.c. and were overwhelmed at their interest in, what to us, was "our job", many visitors returning again and again, often bringing with them, their friends, to whom they wished to introduce the Lt. House. and its' keepers. Guest House proprietors recommended to their guests that they pay us a visit and would often phone to tell us how much it had been enjoyed. Trinity House imposed no charge on visitors to the Lighthouse, and emphasising that it was solely at the Duty Keepers discretion that visitors be admitted. It was not uncommon however, for a grateful member of the public to offer a tip in appreciation, and some schools even sent cheques to be donated to a maritime charity of the host Keepers' choice. As our numerous visitor books showed, our efforts were more than appreciated by our visitors, and it was a sad day when, in 1992 the Lighthouse was automated and therefore had to close to the public permanently. It may seem a somewhat unusual role for the Lighthouse Keeper to play, but I myself derived great personal pleasure in both meeting the public, and in imparting to them, just what goes behind, or rather below, making the light shine out its' reassuring beam. Numerous schools ,walking groups, and other organisations, came to visit, although with larger parties it became necessary for us to organise a system of booking, there being only limited space within the tower! It was interesting to note that even on the wildest of days of winter, there were always some visitors, who, despite the mile long trek, were pleased at being able to inspect the Lt House before automation forced it's closure, many returning time and again, bringing with them friends or relations on a day out. Media interest grew, and soon we were featured on local television and radio with the result that visitor numbers swelled even more! The difficulty came, when, as automation work within the tower became more intensive, we were obliged, essentially for reasons of safety, to curtail our opening hours; however, by good humoured negotiation with the engineers, we still managed to ensure that public interest was satisfied.

To reflect on one of Start Points' lighter moments, (no pun intended); the following occurance,a though amusing now, wasn't quite so at the time !

It was a particularly hot summers' afternoon, and even by Start Points' normally steady stream of visitor numbers, perhaps too hot for anything except perhaps visiting the beach. A few of our more senior citizens had ventured down to see us and enjoy the comparative cool of the tower, but young people were conspicuous by their absence; all, that is, except for two! There was I, at the entrance base quietly browsing some paperwork, when in came; two wet, be draggled teenagers proudly carrying between them a barnacle covered, cylindrical object with fins! They eagerly informed me they had discovered it at the foot of the cliffs between us, and the nearby village of Hallsands. It didn't take any prolonged inspection to reach the conclusion that what they had so proudly delivered to us was so obviously some kind of bomb! After unceremoniously dropping it on the stone floor of the Lighthouse, they explained that they had brought it to us, as we would know just what to do with it! Ideas abounded! They went on to add that there was another identical model lying near to the location of the first, adding, that they would gladly return and collect it! Not a good idea, was my response, whilst trying not to appear over angry,

94

or anxious at what to them, had been an act of supreme public spiritedness.With that ,they left, leaving me to ponder the prospect of Start Point Lighthouse becoming Great Britains' first serious entry into the space race, a situation made worse by no-one on station ever having been trained for space travel ! Least of all, yours truly. Having first tactfully evacuated the tower of our visitors, and exhibited the "closed for emergency maintenance" sign on the gate, I set about transporting the object to the farthest point away from all buildings, almost down at sea level, before alerting the Bomb Disposal team. On inspection, they deemed the object to be a live, and set about rendering it safe prior taking it away for final disposal, returning the next day to locate the remaining device that our bomb delivery boys had mentioned. It was later that week that we received a phone call from those same boys eager to find out if it really had been a bomb of some kind, and still with no real idea that their actions, though exercised with good intent, were, to say the least, foolhardy.

It was not uncommon for explosive devices of all kinds to be found from time to time in and around Start Bay, as much military practice took place there during World War two. Much has recently been written of this, mainly American, activity, which took place as a rehearsal for the D.Day landings, and for which, the South Hams, as the area is geographically known, played a large part, the local population evacuating their homes for many of the years of hostilities. Whilst at Start Point, I to delved through station records to try to learn more of life at the actual Lighthouse under American "occupation", but, apart from mention being made of damage to the gatepost by an American truck, I found very little worthy of record.

Among our many visitors to Start Point, it was not uncommon to meet ex-servicemen from the armed forces, mainly naval, who had wartime experience of patrol duties on the, often stormy waters off Start. It was a joy to share their reminiscences, and they themselves were delighted at being able to look out on a sea that had once been so hostile and dangerous.

One of the most difficult and dangerous tasks encountered by the automation team at Start Pt was the demolition and safe disposal of the old Fog -signal & Engine Room which perched precariously on the increasingly eroding cliff-edge. This task had to be achieved solely by labour intensive means, the rock strata being far too unstable to allow the usage of any type of explosive, or any mechanical equipment liable to cause heavy vibration. So acute was the erosive nature of Start Pt, that serious questions were raised as to the future of a navigational light on the headland, and preliminary alternative sites and arrangements discussed, including the possibility of siting a large tri-pod mounted lamp several hundred yards inland of the existing tower. Fortunately, following successful demolition of the old Fog-signal/engine room site, and a favourable geographical survey, the cliff was professionally stabilised, and Start Point remains, thus far, in it's original profile. There  remains however, a very real long term threat of cliff erosion, particularly from the prevailing wind side (SW) of the point; it therefore being considered prudent to monitor closely, any tell-tale signs of movement in the structure of buildings e.t.c. At relevant areas throughout the Lt Hse station, Geologists have installed warning instruments at the request of Trinity House which, at the time of writing, assure us that, at least for the foreseeable future, Start Point will be there as a guardian sentinel for the mariner, and a focal point for visitors, be it only from the outside, for a long time to come. Who knows, it is only to be hoped that, maybe at some point in the future, and with ever-growing interest in our heritage, the Lighthouse might once again reopen for all to enjoy. At Christmas 1992,with automation work completed, control of Start Point was handed over to the Trinity House Operations Control Centre at Harwich, thus ending a manned history begun in 1862. South Devons' southernmost point is now in the care of the silicon chip, with a locally based attendant visiting on a regular basis to visually check and maintain station navigational aids and safe security.

I left Start Point, in October 1992, having been Keeper in Charge for some months, it became my responsibility to hand over control to a skeleton crew on station; their job being, to ensure that, during the trial period of automatic operation, all equipment behaved according computers' instructions .As a general point, I feel it only correct to state that it was not uncommon, during initial "running-in" periods, for the Base Station to register an alarm or equipment malfunction, when, in reality, in situ, all was functioning normally. Having a. crew on station during this trial period has proved time and again the most efficient and cost effective way of ensuring that, in practice, the highest standards are maintained throughout the automation and de manning process. This is particularly appropriate in the case of off-shore stations where the logistical cost of simply "getting there" i.e .by helicopter, is a high contributor to an already hard pressed budget, and it was at my next station, the Lizard, that I was able to renew my aquaintance with Trinity House helicopters, which, not having flown since my days at Casquets,I welcomed with enthusiasm.

The Lizard, being a control, station, was responsible for the monitoring and maintenance of the "Western Rock" stations comprising of Wolf, Longs hips, Round Island, Bishop Rock lighthouses, and the Sevenstones Light-vessel.( N.B. It was in 1967, on the Sevenstones reef that the tanker "Torrey Canyon" foundered causing large scale oil pollution to the S.W. region.)

,As new technology was introduced to the Lighthouses, so, we, their crews, needed to adapt accordingly, thereby heralding another new series of training courses. Personally ,I have always enjoyed any form of offered training ,and in, particular, relished the opportunity of learning, at least a little, of this new computer age .There were those, however ,especially some of the older generation, who ,(and who could blame them), had no real desire to be anywhere close to any Lighthouse that required a keyboard to make it work!

Automation ,by definition, relied almost entirely upon the computer and the silicon chip. Initially, off shore stations were first on the list for demanning and automation ,not least because, they were the most expensive to man ,service ,and maintain ; anything at all to do with stations offshore, required the use of either helicopter or ship.

Offshore stations, once automated, were remotely monitored by usually ,the geographically closest shore station ,i.e .Lizard, in control of Bishop Rock, Wolf ,e.t.c ,with the crew complements being increased, in order to cover the extra duties that were now required of such stations. As appropriate, perhaps due to breakdown or general inspections, members of the Base station crew would attend their offshore charges, often staying aboard for up to 48hrs.Whilst being stationed at Lizard during 1992/4,I was required to visit our offshore group lights on numerous occasions and enjoyed the experience and responsibility, the training in new technology with which we were increasingly dealing , added a new dimension to our role.I had joined the service and seen the last of the oil burners,(I.O.B) and, in such a relatively short time period ,now saw the Keepers themselves becoming superceded by electronics .On reflection ,throughout my service, there had been continuing change and modernisation, with computerisation playing an increasing role. Because of this ,we, the newest ,and youngest in the Lighthouse Service ,found ourselves with a continuing need to adapt and learn, whereas the older generation had seen the Service change little until very late on in their service careers, when perhaps their inclination  to want to change accordingly was diminished.

Transfer to Lizard Lighthouse called for newly aquired skills to be quickly brought into play; we had been trained in the "new technology" which was now being applied to our lighthouses as they were the converted from manual (Keeper) control, to being controlled via keyboard and a computer screen. For myself, I was pleased to have the opportunity to learn how to operate a computer, which, itself, was in control of a cupboard full of electronics somewhere over the horizon! As part of the next phase in total automation of all our lighthouses, Lizard was one of four monitor stations strategically located within the range of offshore lights. This localized control was a first step to finally being able to monitor and control all UK lighthouses from one central computer base. Whilst monitoring automated stations, in our charge we continued to operate, and manually watch over our own Lizard light in the "old traditional way."

Our crew complement was two crews of four keepers each working four weeks on/off in much the same way as we had operated offshore. As manned stations became less in number, and with keepers and families still living on shore stations such as Lizard, it was decided to encourage and assist all to take up residence in private sector housing. Trinity House were very mindful of the possibility of keepers becoming virtually homeless should this potential problem not be addressed sooner rather than later .As families therefore vacated stations, then these stations became "bachelor status" manned.

Our compliment number at Lizard enabled us to also attend the offshore lights in our charge for maintenance works; this could find any one of us being offshore for one to two days at a time. It was an interesting and varied system of duties which, personally I enjoyed a great deal, although landing on stations that were no longer "lived in" was a strange and eerie experience. No more the sweet aroma of the coffee pot as it hissed and bubbled on the rayburn stove, and the warm greeting of those on station, their personalities positively glowing, their duty turn over now that the relief crew had arrived!

As with most lighthouses within my remit, I had served at Lizard back in SAK times so was familiar with the geography; a five minute stroll was all it took to pick up a daily paper! Now finding myself appointed to Lizard for what would probably be up to three years, I was more than pleased with my posting. To enable further exploration, and in an effort to keep fit, I took my bicycle, when not on duty, I ventured off along the country lanes of the area; it was the perfect way to unwind and will always remain a fond memory. In high summer, with the increased traffic all trying to reach the Lizard and enjoy Englands' southernmost point, cycle transport was by far the fastest and easiest method of "nipping up the village" The Lizard, was, by any standards, a good posting, and one which I was reluctant to leave when the time came.I enjoyed all Lighthouses during my service, but, as with anything in life, favourite experiences and places, can always be called to mind.

As technology advanced within the service, and, in particular with the arrival of computers, the need to learn new skills became even more apparent. In the earlier lighthouse automations ,it was usual to computer monitor one or more unmanned offshore stations, from a geographically convenient manned shore station, i.e. Casquets became monitored by Alderney Lt Hse, some seven miles away. Should a problem occur on the automated light, then members of the monitor station crew would be called upon to visit and further assess or rectify the fault. My transler from Start Pt to Lizard, found me sitting in front of a computer,and overseeing the status of stations which, to me, seemingly not many years previously, had been part of my service as fully manned stations;now, they were all, just data on a VDU screen. We knew everything that was happening on a storm swept rock from the comfort of a chair in a centrally heated room. This felt, initially, somewhat eerie, and difficult to fully take in. Reading the screen for Wolf Rock, for example, brought to mind tales of long overdue reliefs, of weeks waiting for suitable weather in which to send in a boat; of seas crashing over the lighthouse roof top, as if to completely ignore the efforts of those Victorian engineers who had, against the odds, established themselves as masters of a piece of weed covered rock which itself,had claimed so many ships and lives over the centuries. Now, all just figures and lights on a screen; ghosts to travel the ether as signals sent to and from a base station, many miles away.

At Lizard being a busy monitor station, We had a complement of eight, divided into two crews each of four, each duty crew working 4 weeks on/off. Whilst operating Lizard as a watched light in the traditional way, we also now had responsibility for the "out stations" within our charge. Our watch keeping system and hours were, as with any other station, except that every third and forth days were regarded as "standby days" on which we could, and usually were, required to attend our off shore charges. This could involve being on station for perhaps just a few hours or, frequently, stays of up to 48 hours. Taken out by helicopter, we would, in teams of two, effect a regular maintenance schedule and carry out routine manual checks on all of the stations systems.

Whenever any other maintenance trade was visiting the Lighthouse, the ruling was always that a trained Keeper should accompany them on station; security of the station after such a visit was solely the Keepers, responsibility, and, prior to leaving the station, all systems had to be reverted to full computer control at Lizard. This was achieved by radio liason with the duty Keeper monitoring the procedure, as, one by one, each item of station equipment was switched back into the care of the silicon chip.

It is my belief that the tower structures were just the body of a lighthouse, but that it was the Lighthouse Keepers that formed its' soul. Our brief visits on maintenance duties could not, ever recapture the way it had once been. The lighthouse had now become guardian to panels of electronics, there to obey a person with a keyboard a long way away.

# SECTION FOUR
## CAREER REFLECTIONS AND FINAL POSTING

During my two and a half years SAK service ,I did duty on some 20 different stations, returning to some on several occasions.

This kind of travelling lifestyle was, in its, own way quite exciting. At no other time during ones' career, was it likely that one would get to visit such a variety of different places and lighthouses. For myself ,visiting the Isles of Scilly(for Bishop Rock and Round Island )was a particularly valued opportunity, as was going to completely uninhabited islands ,uninhabited that is, except for the lighthouse keepers ;the island of Flatholm in the Bristol Channel ,provided such an adventure.

Flatholm ,steeped in history had remnants of its 'past all over the island ,ruined buildings, including a former cholera hospital where inbound Bristol shipping would embark those so afflicted before being allowed to enter port. An almost intact Victorian garrison was there to be explored, as was the parade ground and the once proud cannon, now lying rusting away. Around the coasts of England and Wales there are many such islands with no other occupants except for those at the lighthouse; such places remain untouched by developers nor spoilt by vandals. To be afforded the opportunity to spend time on such places, was, to me, priceless and a rare gift committed to my memory for always .It is a widely held perception that the Lighthouse Keepers' life was made up of dull, monotonous routine, with the term ,boring, frequently expressed. My response, a resounding, "Never!"

We all have a mental picture as to just what a lighthouse looks like, and our individual perceptions probably differ little between us. There are, however, exceptions to that of the "normal" style and appearance of lighthouses; by this, I refer to the Nab Tower Lighthouse which is to be found about eight miles from the eastern most tip of the Isle of Wight, guarding this much used entrance to the ports of Southampton and Portsmouth. The Nab, colliqually referred to as "the leaning tower" is an iron and steel structure which was originally built as part of a first world war chain of anti submarine defence towers. Built on shore, and floated out to it's site, its controlled siting on the sea bed did not go to plan, leaving it in a permanently listing position.

The Nab Tower had some six floors, with only the topmost "penthouse suite" forming the Lighthouse Keepers quarters, the lower floors being occupied by the Royal Navy. In my time of service on station, the R.N areas which included generator rooms, bedrooms, galley and a small hospital area, were all "mothballed" and out of service, with we, the keepers having access for caretaking inspections. I have to admit to becoming lost during my first exploration of this mysterious structure, but also to thoroughly enjoying the adventure!

Reliefs for the Nab were conducted via the Trinity House Pilots at Ryde, I.O W, whose craft were in our area serving the shipping needs throughout the day and night; for us, it meant regular mail and paper deliveries every few days, a much valued amenity! The outer area surrounding the tower was served by a large verandah type deck, much favoured by us for off duty sun bathing or circuit walks for exercise. There was, however, one aspect of the Nab Tower that simply has to be quite unique, that is that with a leaning tower, comes sloping floors! Under each piece of furniture, (i.e. the table ), could be found blocks of wood placed at one end to level it up! I often thought how even I, could be an excellent snooker player should we have had a table; as even I could not have failed to pot all the requires balls into a corner pocket!

The fog horn was compressed air driven and operated in a similar way to most other stations except that the Nab's fog horn was assisted in its' work by a large fog bell on the roof. In between each blast from the fog horn came a loud "dong" from the bell; sleeping in the room immediately underneath it I couldn't help but think how not content with just the brass section, we had now aquired an orchestra!

The navigation lights, of which there were two, were each housed in a man size tower, one on each of the North and South sides of the roof; although electrically powered via the station generators, the revolving optics were propelled by clockwork and required to be wound every two hours during service.

Situated in deep water with no immediate navigational hazards meant that deliveries of water and essential supplies could be effected by Trinity House tender moored alongside the tower itself. Having done duty at Needles Lighthouse, and then, following a months leave, then transferred to Nab, I was then able to experience the variety of Solent shipping from each end of the Isle of Wight. Whilst the Needles channel was frequented by some very large ships, particularly ocean liners, this access to Southampton was only of use to such vessels during, mainly spring high tides; whereas the Nabs' much deeper channel, remained accessable at almost any tidal state. Some of the largest shipping afloat entered Southampton Water via the Nab channel, such vessels towering above our "leaning lighthouse" as they passed, often very closely, by.

I recall, how, due to a public holiday and an apparent industrial dispute at Southampton docks, shipping arriving at Nab, was required to wait at anchor until berthing was available. At one point, there were seven huge container vessels "parked" just off our station, their deck tannoys playing music to the crews working out on deck.(and also to us !!!!) Much as I enjoy music of most tastes, I cannot, nor ever have, been able to sing along to Japanese pop songs!

One Principal Keeper, Eric, sadly no longer with us, was an avid ship photographer who regularly submitted pictures to shipping enthusiasts publications. One afternoon, a large Soviet freighter, with hammer and sickle emblazoning its funnel, drew ever closer to the lighthouse; on the wing of the bridge a gathering of sailors could clearly be seen taking in the view of our English coastline in fine summers weather. As the vessel was about to pass, almost underneath our site, Eric lined up his camera. In a matter of seconds, the small group of sailors previously assembled, had ran into the wheelhouse and shut the door behind them! They clearly were intent on not having their photographs taken  thank you!

This incident took place in 1976, at a time when we were still in the cold war uncertainties and we in the lighthouses were tasked, as part of our duties, to report certain identified classes of eastern bloc shipping; our freighter, incidently, was not such a vessel!

Duty on the Nab Tower was, yet another, valued experience, and having, during my SAK service, visited twice, still found new areas to explore. Because there were only we keepers in residence, water supply was virtually unlimited, the storage being designed to cope with a full compliment which included Naval and Trinity House personnel. We received frequent visits from the Royal Naval Auxillary vessel, "Waterwitch," which was often in our area servicing warships. On her way returning to base at Portsmouth, and having water etc left on board, they would call in and off load a few gallons.

Prior to going away on a duty turn, part of the routine was a visit to the hairdresser to ensure the requisite uniform shortness of hair, but, at times, especially when away for longer than normal periods, ones' hair needed further attention with the scissors!

On Nab Tower, this was not a problem as, one of the keepers, whom I shall simply call Neville, was very adept as a Barber and had all the necessary clippers etc with which to do the job!

Having booked ones haircut, Neville would proceed to the flag locker, and return with a full size Trinity House Ensign. He would then drape the flag over ones shoulders and proceed with his scissors. Though he was not a qualified hairdresser, Neville was as good a Barber as could be found anywhere! A wonderful time, remembered with affection!

Early in my career just a few short months after joining, I was despatched to Anvil Point, a shore station at Swanage in Dorset It being July, and, with the lighthouse station situated in country parkland, it immediately struck me as being absolutely idyllic .I had found, as a travelling SAK ,that some shore stations were less popular than others, the main reason resting on the fact that many such lighthouses were quite some distance from the nearest village or shop, a five mile walk was not uncommon. A Keeper, perhaps taking a car, had no difficulty, but, as the majority of relieving keepers(SAKs), did not, their isolation was obvious.

Trinity House provided all shore stations with a contract shopping taxi, this amenity being mainly for the benefit of keepers wives on station, would, on a weekly basis, take them to the nearest town for shopping visits. Any other keepers on station, ie, SAKs, were to be included on the trip should they wish to go, I, personally found the facility more than useful.

Anvil Point was not only in a beautiful area, but, was also easily accessible to town and amenities; a short enjoyable stroll took one to the centre of town in less than 15 minutes. That, coupled with the sight and sound of so much wildlife, made the lighthouse station more than eligible for my "Good Lt Hse guide! To be up in the lantern in early morning just after dawn, it was my pleasure on more than one occasion to see a herd of Deer just up the hillside from the lighthouse; the sight of a large stag silhouetted against the early morning sky makes an awesome and unforgettable sight. My personal lighthouse preferences, however, have always rested with the offshore rock stations, not least, because of the time off factor, ie. one month on/off once appointed. On a more personal note, on joining the Service, we were fortunate in owning our home, and therefore had no wish to give it up and take up Trinity House accommodation. Service in the Rock lights gave us the opportunity to both keep our home, and also to have every other month clear of duty in which to enjoy it.

As both an SAK, and later serving as a pool keeper, I served on many shore stations as a relief. On such stations, the quarters provided for the single keeper comprised a flatlet, or suite of rooms (bedroom ,lounge/kitchen and bathroom) and were very well appointed for the purpose. At the end of each stay by a relieving keeper, all facilities had to be thoroughly cleaned and made ready for the next possible in comer. Before one departing station, the quarters were inspected and passed ok by the Principal Keeper on station. By so doing, one could always rely upon good standards of accommodation, and be assured that all relevant services, ie fridge etc, were all in good order.

Although, on most occasions, one would be the only relieving keeper on station ,at times there could be two SAKs sharing; this not only providing company, but also often meant being able to share chores, such as, on alternate days, the cooking also!

As an SAK at Lizard, and later at Anvil Pt, with only myself in residence in the quarters, I was pleased to be able to have my wife stay with me for a week or so on station; when I was off duty, we were able to enjoy some pleasant walks along the coast paths, almost as though we were on holiday! It also gave my wife an insight ,at first hand, into the working of a lighthouse, even to the point of sharing some night watches with me, and ensuring that I was well supplied with the essential cups of coffee! Both my wife, and myself enjoyed her short insight into lighthouse life and fondly recall that privileged opportunity.

The tower at Anvil Pt was extremely short! Just one short stairway took one to the top; this made the cleaning routine a simple task, particularly following an afternoon of conducting visitors around the lighthouse, as, in line with most other land stations, Anvil was open to the public during summer afternoons. .The station fog signal, was electric, its' sound being "polite" and directed seawards. Having only ever previously experienced the (loud!!) air driven fog horns, to enjoy quality sleep time, even in foggy conditions, I found to be quite a novelty ! Yet another reason for Anvil Point finding its, way into my "good lighthouse guide!"

The end of manned lighthouses came as a gradual process for me; as and when a new provisional redundancy date was known, Trinity House made certain that all keepers were made aware of any new arrangements. At Trinity House expense, training courses could be taken up as an addition to ones' personal skills base, to aid future employment prospects when redundancy demanded! We were also offered courses in personal financial management in order to ensure the best use of our pensions and severance package gratuities. With some of the manpower taking voluntary redundancy, then, this factor delayed the enforced redundancy of those of us who preferred to stay. Needless to say ,rumours abounded , but to the credit of T.H, all information was freely available to all, thus greatly reducing the "grapevine factor"

My projected date for departure from the service was given to me as Spring 1996, and, with this in mind, I was transferred from Lizard Lighthouse to Portland Bill Lighthouse in September 1995. Portland Bill was already entering the preliminary stages of conversion to automatic status when I arrived; completion being anticipated as being at or by March '96.

I had, on several occasions as an SAK, seen service at Portland, and with the present Lighthouse tower being the third such lighthouse structure to serve the headland, there was much lighthouse history to explore. As at Lizard, I had taken my trusty mountain bike with me; being reasonably close to the local community shops and library etc, this was an invaluable asset and way of keeping fit!

In my final weeks of service at Portland, I was able to take some video footage of the automation works in progress, as well as revisit the other two, now redundant towers, in an effort to put a further perspective on what was to be the final chapter of lighthouse keeping at Portland. It all began to feel final, just knowing that yet another of our well known, traditional lighthouses, was going the way of the silicon chip; this time, however, it was taking me with it! No more lights to run (transfer) to, after 22 years, this was really it! Whilst exploring the previous lights of Portland, and taking my video record of the automation, it crossed my mind how, from the old lights, keepers had merely moved further along the headland and resettled into a new one, probably proud to be a part of the new station with everything brand new and up to the minute. This time, the keepers themselves, including myself, were going too!

And so it was, that at 0415 on a cold February morning in 1996, I left Portland Bill and the Lighthouse Service ; I had completed my final watch 0000-0400 and with a heavy heart, proceeded homewards. It was actually June of that year, following the taking of time expired leave etc before my service was finalised. A sad, but proud end.

On the" lighter side." A selection of smile worthy episodes in my lighthouse life .

My career in Trinity House Lighthouse Service involved working within a strict routine of ordered duties essential for the safe and efficient operation of the lighthouse and its' navigational aids. The lighthouse team of keepers needed to' bond together to achieve this aim, yet, at the same time, called for a certain sense of good humour in order to help those, often long days and nights of isolated living. During the course of duty, incidents occurred which, even today, I look back upon with a grin!

It had often been a sense of wonder to me, as to just how far, messages in bottles, had ,throughout history, travelled; this thought led me to want to try one for myself! With two bottles, each containing the Needles lighthouse contact address, were, with due ceremony, dispatched into the will the outgoing tide, which, off Needles; can be a very strong current. Within a week, I received forty seven individual letters from the pupils of a Primary school just across the Solent near Bournemouth, a mere five miles or so away! A young boy, on the beach with his parents, had found my bottle message, and, having proudly taken it to school; his teacher; .seeing it a good class project, had invited the class 'to each write a letter to the lighthouse keeper" over there on Needles!"

I found their letters to be wonderfully inspirational, and their thoughts on life as a Keeper to be most entertaining; in addition to the usual lighthouse questions, there were comments like, "your job must be goodto do because you can get away from your wife a lot!". We, (and my wife!) roared with laughter at their letters and their, . thoughts on lighthouse life.

Receiving letters from so many children, average, age eight to nine; made me resolved to reply, there always seeming to me something special in the way that children see things, especially their thoughts regarding lighthouses and lighthouse. keepers! It was only when starting to write, that I realised that I would have to scribe forty seven individual replies, and, whilst trying to vary the letter contents! I eventually completed the task. Courtesy of Trinity House public relations section, I was pleased to be able to forward some lighthouse information and pictures etc, back to the children and their school!. It became a beautiful friendship between the keepers and that school, with the exchange of Xmas cards and wishes becoming a regular part of our lives.

Oh, and the other bottle? Slightly better luck distance wise, in that we received a letter from a German family, who, whilst holidaying in Denmark, had found my bottle and replied. I sent them a selection of English stamps together with a picture postcard of Needles together with my thanks. The bottle had been in the water for almost a full year prior to its' discovery!

Having a mind to sea pollution, and being more than aware of the state of our oceans, these two message in a bottle episodes, were my only such attempts. I considered that, with both bottles having been retrieved, and in the hope that their finders, once having removed the contents, would have placed the then empty bottles in the appropriate bin, I could never be considered a major pollution source!

# WHAT LURKS BENEATH

Tower rock lighthouses differ in height, basic outline shape, etc, but, in their general interior layout, they share several similarities, not least in areas set aside for storage of utilities, i.e. water.

The main water storage tank at Needles lighthouse, as at most stations, was immediately beneath the base floor, in fact, almost within the base rock itself; the tower having been constructed in 1879 meant that the tank, at that time would have been underneath a storeroom. As "new" technology arrived at the lighthouse, generator engines came to be installed within the former store room, and for well over fifty years or more, the room became the main engine/plant room for the station. Upon my being stationed at Needles from 1977, we had four diesel engine sets, all situated on the floor immediately above the main freshwater tank, access to which was via a "manhole" type cover within the floor.

It was during the summer of 1980, that we began to notice that our drinking water had a taint to it, which, upon closer analysis, showed that a slight oily tinge was present within it. Professional inspection by Portsmouth Health Authority confirmed that our supply had indeed become contaminated by oil pollution, rendering it unfit for consumption. Trinity House immediately instigated a programme of tank cleaning and purification to be carried out by Trinity House tender crews. The tank, capacity 1500 gallons, was treated and flushed out over and over until deemed to be clear by professional analysts ashore. During this operation, our local boatman, Tony, delivered fresh water to us on a daily basis; fortunately the weather remained kind to us to enable this to be effected. Despite the best efforts of Trinity House, over a further period of weeks, the contamination returned, the granite rock of the water tank had obviously become porous and was allowing the ingress of years of built up engine oil and fuel seepage. A decision was made to line the interior of the tank with a non permeous fibre glass skin, and a contract was awarded to a firm oflaminators from nearby Poole, just across the water.

Two tradesmen laminators lived with us on station for just over a week whist they installed a beautiful duck egg blue coloured lining within the ten foot deep tank.As they proudly showing us their efforts on completion, we could not fail to notice their surprise gift to us; lining the tank bottom were a whole host of "centre spread" topless women pictures, obviously "borrowed" from a men only magazine! Laminated in clear resin, their images became enlarged as thetank was slowly refilled from the visiting ship whose crew thought it hilarious, {privately, so did we!).As the water level increased, then so did the bust sizes of the young ladies whose pictures graced our water tank! We came to be able to gauge the amount of water left by using a simple equation based upon what we saw staring up at us through the crystal clear water.

Following automation, the water tanks use was changed to that of diesel storage thus obscuring the view of any images. I see no reason to doubt that they still remain on station, and, who knows, someone in the far future might discover them and forever ponder as to just how what lurks beneath came to be there and why!

The very last lighthouse, North Foreland, was automated in 1998, and, to commemorate the passing of manned lights, a service of thanksgiving was held at St Olaves' Church in London. This was followed by a reception at Trinity House during which medallions were presented to all Lighthouse Keepers by Prince Philip, HRH The Duke of Edinburgh, Master of Trinity House. I feel privileged to have served in the Trinity House Lighthouse Service, and view my medal with the pride I know I will always hold.

My interest in maritime heritage allowed me to persue my lighthouse times with enjoyment, further to which, I have found myself lecturing on life on Lighthouses ; each one talk bringing requests from other groups and societies; the year 2007 found me at the London Boat Show telling my story. This was, to me, my single most charismatic lecture so far, and I still wonder, whilst being extremely proud to do it, how I got to be invited to speak at such a venue! Such, obviously, is the level of interest in lighthouses and their heritage.

The lighthouse keeper is unique, and sadly, represents an occupation, of which no one will be left to tell the story first hand. It is my hope that both by talking of just what it was like, and committing the experience to paper, that, when someone points out to sea at a lighthouse tower, now no longer lived in, they will have been able to learn, from first hand experiences, just what was involved in its, operation pre silicon chip!

For me, the lighthouse story will probably never close as long as I still have the health and strength to tell it; I recall to mind little anecdotes of my off shore life, and often think back to happenings out on the light, wondering how so and so is now ? what ever happened to whoever? The Association of Lighthouse Keepers and its, magazine helps with its, tales of yore sent in by those, who, just like me, hold those times as precious. Trinity House also publishes our house magazine, and, interesting though it is, sadly so often contains sad news regarding ones, former colleagues all of whom played their part in our Lighthouse history .I have, more recently had the pleasure of being invited to assist in reopening Start Point Lighthouse to the public, and, on occasions have myself conducted tours, in addition to helping train the regular Tour Guiding staff as to just how our "Hands made the Lights work"

So, looking back over my Lighthouse Service career, and , using perhaps, the aid of a little hindsight, just what had it meant to me personally, to have spent all those years couped up, often far from land, yet going nowhere?

I have often been asked, by friends and others of the general public, just what was it that instilled me to even consider such a career? They have always seen me as an outgoing, social person, who really enjoys the company of others; in that, I would not disagree, and, I suppose, in some ways I have even surprised myself! To share the companionship of even just two other men , to me became something special. To me, it mattered not what (if any) was their chosen faith, nor their politics or choice of football team, to me, they were simply my team, without whom, particularly when I came to be in charge, our lighthouse station just could not function. No matter what the chore, or need, we were always able to carry out our duties with a smile, and more often than not, a real laugh! I, a former seaman, was a long way from home, sharing a small space with, maybe a former butcher, electrician, and, at one time, even with a former underground train driver! Contrary to popular belief, a nautical background was not an obligatory requisite for entry into the service, what was most important, apart from a reasonable level of education, was self reliance and an ability to get on with ones' fellow man, often under conditions of stress.

My entry into the service found me on the initial SAK Training course with nine other entrants; by the end of the first year, only three of us remained in service, each of us staying the full career distance until "automation of lighthouses" did us part. It seemed to be a career in which anyone who felt doubtful of it, was soon out, interestingly by resignation rather than at the request of Trinity House. It was, apparently a similar scenario in the case of Trinity House, Blackwall, out station mechanics and others. I am the first to accept that, whilst it suited me, to many others, not being able to, perhaps attend a Saturday football match, or play darts at the local on a Friday, was too much to bear. Others, I know found that their loved ones at home, suffered stress as result of their menfolk being away; for myself, I will always be thankful to my own wife for her support in my Lighthouse career, without such support, I too, might have had to think again. Perhaps those of us from a sea faring background, and our families may have found it just a little easier than those whose partners had always previously arrived home for tea at five o'clock, and now found themselves apart at Xmas. None the less, from whatever background, it mattered not to the rest of us, as, the fellowship bond which grew from our isolation, grew to become special. Each man knew the others likes, dislikes, and most importantly, the others job. If one felt **ill** on station, I recall once having the flu, the other two doubled up on their watches, left me in bed, and regularly served me with tea and paracetamols, until I was fit to return to my watches.

There is nothing that I would have changed in my Lighthouse Keeping career, except that I would have began it sooner! If I could have my time over again, then I would do it again; I can offer no better accolade than simply that.

# POSTSCRIPT AND
# FURTHER INFORMATION

Further information on Lighthouses and their Keepers contact:

Trinity House. www.trinityhouse.gov.uk

Association of Lighthouse Keepers. www.alk.org.uk

Information on Lighthouse Accommodation available for holiday letting: Link from:  www.alk.org.uk

Information regarding Lighthouses open to public.
www.trinityhouse.gov.uk

To  Contact me, Gordon Partridge: thelighthousekeeper@fsmail.net

Printed in Great Britain
by Amazon.co.uk, Ltd.,
Marston Gate.